Nail That Job

The complete guide for the
less-experienced jobseeker

SIAN CASE

This is for J. and A.
May all their future careers be glittering.

I would particularly like to thank the many hundreds of jobseekers I have worked with over the years, especially the few who share their stories anonymously here for you to learn from.

Thanks also to Sarah Constable and Joyce Mason from Inkwell Media Ltd, Susan Archer, Kathryn Dobbie, Jess Fidler, Ruth Hawksworth, Jane Heaton, Chris Johnson and John Wade.

Special thanks to Bill for all the tea and perspective and Yvonne for all the common sense.

For further advice and personalised support, please visit
www.nailthatjob.co.uk

Designed and produced by Inkwell Media Limited

9 Lancaster Centre, Meteor Business Park
Staverton GL2 9QL

www.inkwellmedia.co.uk

ISBN 978-0-9560859-9-3

CONTENTS

INTRODUCTION: How to use this book

If you are reading this then you fall into one of the following categories:

> ***You have recently left or are about to leave school, college or university and are looking for your first job.***
>
> ***You are currently employed and dissatisfied in some way with your job, which you have held for some time.***
>
> ***You are between jobs, currently out of work (the acting profession call it 'resting') and have been looking for your next role for some time.***

Whatever your position in the job market and whatever job role you are looking for in any industry, then please read on for a wealth of tips from an experienced recruiter who trains recruiters and supports jobseekers. This book contains many useful hints and tips that have already proved effective for job hunters from a wide variety of industries and job roles. It has been specially designed to guide the less-experienced jobseeker who may be feeling a little overwhelmed by the scale of work needed to succeed in the modern job market.

You can dip in and out of key chapters, depending on how far you have already come on your job search journey. However, you will get the most out of this book by working through all of the exercises in the right order. It is structured to take you through the entire job search process. We will explore:

- What you really want and need from your next paid employment.
- How to identify and describe clearly your many talents.
- How to maximise your time researching the right industries, organisations and potential jobs.
- How to present yourself strongly on CVs and application forms.
- How to prepare effectively for all kinds of selection procedures.
- How to make the best impact you can at the start of the next stage of your career.

At key points in the book, you will find activities that prompt you to reflect on your personal job search and create raw material for real applications. Jobseekers I have coached tell me how helpful they find these reflections to clarify their job search aims. Please complete all the questions in as much detail as you can when you work through the exercises – you will truly get the most out of this book by putting in as much as you can.

After having read this book and applied the key learning points, you will be able to:

- Focus your job search to find a meaningful new role that will suit your current experience well and develop your skills further.
- Present your unique mix of skills and abilities accurately and attractively to find a job that is the right match for you.

You will enjoy your next job because it will offer you the right mix of demands and experiences for this point in your career. It will also connect strategically with the rest of your career, even if it is a temporary post. You will either be in the ideal job for you or the job that is the correct next step towards your ideal job.

No job can ever be guaranteed to be safe but the safest jobholders are those who remain clear about their contribution to their organisation and can demonstrate their worth to their employers. After reading this book, **you** will be that person.

Sian Case
www.nailthatjob.co.uk

P.S. *Please drop us a line at* **sian@nailthatjob.co.uk** *to share your success stories when you nail that ideal job. We love hearing from all our readers about their triumphs and celebrations.*

CHAPTER 1 Know who you are ... and what you want

By the end of this chapter, you will be able to describe clearly:

- ***What your key strengths are.***
- ***What you are good at, with examples that show what you have achieved.***
- ***What you don't like and why.***
- ***What is important to you at work and why.***
- ***What you want from your next job and what you need from your next job and the difference between the two.***
- ***A summary of what you have to offer and what you are looking for.***

You will also have a deeper understanding of yourself and therefore will be ready to start researching the right job for you.

The fundamental question that you must be able to answer both for yourself and soon for an interviewer is:

> ***Who are you and what are you looking for from your next job and all your subsequent jobs until your retirement?***

Before you even start writing a CV, browsing a website or pick up a paper to look for job advertisements, you need to be able to describe to another person a summary of what you can offer and what you are looking for. Recruiters are confronted daily with poorly prepared applications from jobseekers who have clearly never asked themselves these questions. Particularly when the job market is tough, many people just panic and apply for every job that crosses their path, without considering how relevant that job is to their current career development. Some people end up just bouncing from one unsuitable post to another and take years to wonder why they never feel comfortable at work or why they never achieve anything meaningful.

TIP
The key learning for NAIL THAT JOB jobseekers is to prize quality above quantity. You will succeed when you focus your energy on applying for the right job in the right way, rather than scattering endless applications to the winds.

Thoughtful jobseekers nail the right job at each point of their career development and so reach retirement able to reflect on a progressive career that has given them positive learning experiences and a sense of satisfaction. The good news is that all of us, at every stage of our careers, can find and nail the right job by researching thoroughly what we have to offer our next employer and which roles out there in the labour market best fit our current mix of skills and abilities.

■ Who are you?

This is not such a complex, nor as frivolous a question as it may first appear. You are very likely to be asked it during your next job interview *(see Chapter 4, page 116)*, and the recruiter will be expecting a fluent, confident and convincing answer from you. You are the product of all your unique experiences to date, which means that you have a unique set of skills to offer your next employer. Your key purpose when jobseeking is to present clearly and quickly who you are, right from your CV presentation through the complete selection process. When you are asked something along the lines of:

> *"Now, could you start by telling us a bit about yourself please?"*, this is your golden opportunity to present your unique sales pitch.

A helpful start point for describing who you are – and therefore also what you have to offer – is to list all the things that you can do. Consider where you learned these skills and how they may help your next employer. A grid appears on the next page for you to complete. It is not a complete list of all possible competences that any employer could be looking for, but it does cover most of the common experiences that employers want in the modern workplace. A ***competence*** is a quality, skill or ability to do something and recruiters use these descriptions to list what their successful candidates need to be able to do. (Please see the Recruitment Jargon Buster on page 195 for more explanations of technical recruitment terms.) There is no weighting to this list but employers will apply their own weighting depending on the job that you apply for. Different competences will be more or less important for different roles. This is mentioned later in the book when you are assessing which competences may be valued by different companies *(see Chapter 3, page 96)*.

Work through the list and note examples of any situations from your paid or unpaid employment or study where you think that you displayed this competence. If you currently have little paid work experience to draw on, then voluntary work or structured leisure activities are perfectly relevant sources of evidence. Any scale of work will do for collecting examples: what you are doing here is starting to gather evidence that may well end up, polished a little more, on your CV. There is no time limit on how long ago you last practised that competence – all you need to do for the moment is gather as many examples as you can think of to match these descriptions. You will assess them for relevance to your CV in the context of specific applications later.

As you jot down your memories, make a note in the right hand box of what your activity achieved that was of benefit to that employer or, if it was unpaid work, how it helped to complete the task. Helpful measures of success include saving time or money, improving a product or process, reducing waste or errors, improving customer service, increasing sales and improving the experience of the service user or outcome. There are some spare boxes at the end of the competency list for you to add any more that you can think of or, if you are focusing on a specific application, any more competences mentioned in that job description.

Depending on the context of the examples you come up with, you might think that several of these competences appear to overlap. Indeed, expect any example to be relevant for demonstrating more than one competence.

If you can think of more than one example for each competency, you will have a stronger base for building your CV later. By the time you reach an interview to talk about this specific experience, you will have collected a suite of strong examples that mean you should not be repeating the same few anecdotes.

EXERCISE 1: Identifying what I can do

COMPETENCE	EVIDENCE THAT I CAN DO THIS	IMPACT OF USING THIS COMPETENCE
Attention to detail		
Change management		
Communication skills: written and oral		
Creativity		
Customer service		
Data/information analysis		
Decision making		
Design/construct objects		
Driving		

This exercise is continued on following page

COMPETENCE	EVIDENCE THAT I CAN DO THIS	IMPACT OF USING THIS COMPETENCE
Experience of using specific computer programmes		
Flexibility		
Foreign language		
Leadership		
Managing a budget		
Negotiating skills		
Numeracy		
Persistence through difficult circumstances		
Planning and organising		
Presentation skills		
Prioritising		
Problem solving		

COMPETENCE	EVIDENCE THAT I CAN DO THIS	IMPACT OF USING THIS COMPETENCE
Punctuality		
Selling		
Smart appearance		
Teamwork		
Thinking of new ideas		
Time management/ Achieving deadlines		
Using machinery		
Working on my own initiative		
(Please use the boxes below for any additional competencies.)		

What you have just done is identify your ***transferable skills***. Transferable skills are any skills that you have learned to use in one job that could be also applied in other jobs, so they can transfer between different job roles and even different industries. Most of the skills listed in the table above can be used in very different situations: for example, planning and organising always demands the same skills of being able to imagine future events, sequencing them, prioritising, decision making, communicating and problem solving. The scope of work, the final outcome and the detail of specific tasks that you plan differ from job to job, but the core skill remains the same. You may have learned how to plan by preparing next month's work rosters for a team of people, organising a large family wedding, the logistics of a trade exhibition, the village fête or what is required to go in the freezer for next month's family meals. Regardless of the context, you have planned ahead to anticipate everything needed for a successful outcome. In the impact box, consider the most significant result you have achieved from this core skill of planning. It will be helpful to build on when you reach Chapter 3 and start writing your CVs.

CASE STUDY

Demonstrating the benefit of evidencing your transferable skills

Sammy was very bored in a junior administrative job in a large government agency. She had drifted into this job while temping, after graduating with a very specialised degree with limited openings, but did not know how to escape her undemanding job. She started helping out with a Brownie pack – and found that her voluntary work was by far the most rewarding part of her week. As I coached her, she realised that working with children was her true vocation but could not imagine how her current job could offer any meaningful experiences to use in a CV targeting teaching assistant roles.

We worked through Exercise 1 and she was then able to describe several very clear examples of transferable skills such as planning, creativity, achieving deadlines, working on her own initiative, teamwork and prioritising. These skills were learned and applied in a non-school context, but her CV was strong enough to get her a teaching assistant role, which she is now growing into a teaching qualification.

■ Potential motivators

A list of your current skills, abilities and experiences does not completely summarise who you are for a potential employer. They will also be interested in what motivates you at work and may even ask you that question outright at interview. When I ask jobseekers I coach to list what motivates them at work, the first response is frequently, "money". Of course we all need money to eat and keep a roof over our heads, but we get so many other benefits from any type of paid or unpaid employment. Many of us take these benefits for granted until we lose them. After due consideration, most people will admit that money is what gets them out of bed in the morning but other, less tangible, factors prompt them to work harder once they arrive at work.

Have a look at the next list and ponder which experiences are important to you. Some of these things may leave you completely cold or you may never have thought about them having anything to do with what you enjoy at work. Again, there is definitely no right or wrong answer here, just tick what appeals to you and have a go at describing why these things are important to you. This list can be described as a bit 'touchy-feely' – it certainly contains work experiences that are rarely captured in a job description but they can make or break the right job for you.

> *"Money was never a big motivation for me, except as a way to keep score. The real excitement is playing the game."* DONALD TRUMP, American business magnate and author

An example of how I've used this exercise is with auditors. The technical functions of auditing do not change – a national professional qualification demands that every auditor can apply a defined set of skills. However, auditors can be found in very different parts of organisational structures; some thrive on working directly with their customers to help them solve problems collaboratively; others much prefer the thrill of working on their own to generate a solution. The purpose of this exercise is to help you clarify what matters to you in your workplace. It will also clarify what you enjoy about work and – just as importantly – what you don't. These ideas will be developed further in the next exercise. Again, there are a few blank rows at the end of the table for you to add any other motivators that mean a lot to you from your current or last job.

EXERCISE 2: Identifying what is important to me at work

POTENTIAL MOTIVATOR	TICK	THIS IS IMPORTANT TO ME BECAUSE:
Authority to make key decisions		
Being able to make a difference		
Colleagues are also friends		
Comfortable with a routine		
Compliments from colleagues or customers		
Compliments from my boss		
Creativity or innovation is valued		
Delivering good service		
Finding the right answer or solving problems on my own		
Flexible working hours		
Helping colleagues learn new things		
I am challenged		
I am supported		

POTENTIAL MOTIVATOR	TICK	THIS IS IMPORTANT TO ME BECAUSE:
Keeping busy		
Learning new things		
Looking for new projects		
Meeting new people		
Opportunities to work from home		
Pleasant working conditions		
Satisfaction for a job well done		
Selling		
Solving customers' problems		
Status/respect from others		
Staying on my regular site/area		
Talking to customers		
The social scene linked to work		
There's a buzz/ energy/pace to work		

This exercise is continued on following page

POTENTIAL MOTIVATOR	TICK	THIS IS IMPORTANT TO ME BECAUSE:
Travelling		
Tying up all the loose ends		
Visualising the big picture		
Working as part of a large organisation		
Working as part of a team		
Working for a good boss		
Working in an industry that supports my values		
Working in a small organisation		
Working out of doors		
(Please use the boxes below for any additional motivators.)		

Defining what I do and don't enjoy

The next part of this exercise will help you clarify what you are looking for from your next job. Consider your last or current job and reflect for a moment on the work you did/do. Identify what you enjoyed most about this work and what you enjoyed least. If you are young and have only temporary, part-time or voluntary work to consider, please reflect on every job and other experiences, such as studying or hobbies, so that you can throw in as many examples as possible. Incidentally, as you work through this book, you will notice that temporary, part-time and voluntary work will prove very useful for displaying your skills to good advantage for your future employers. Consequently, whenever you see an invitation to reflect on your work experiences, please remember that all experiences are valuable. You may decide that the most valuable next step for your career could be to take a temporary, part-time or voluntary job.

Your next exercise asks you to reflect on your past/current jobs and identify what you want to bring from them into your future roles and what you want to leave behind. You will truly perform at your best for your next employer when you enjoy how you spend your working day, so take the first step now to make the rest of your career rewarding. The grid has headings that simply divide your past/current jobs into aspects for you to comment on. In the middle box, list some specific examples to demonstrate why a particular task, skill, relationship or result is for you: thrilling, satisfying or boring. If you really can't think of any examples, try talking it through with a **trusted** colleague, but the examples you jot down must come from your heart rather than their opinion.

> *"Experience is not what happens to you. It's what you do with what happens to you."* ALDOUS HUXLEY, 20th century author

As you work through the grid, please try to identify as precisely as possible what it is that interests or motivates you about that part of your job. Every job has specific tasks or activities that need to be carried out using a variety of skills, knowledge or experience. Every job demands that you develop productive relationships with someone and that you have an impact on something by the end of the day, otherwise there would be no point in paying you.

EXERCISE 3: Identifying what I like and dislike about work

ASPECTS OF MY JOB	POSITIVE THINGS ABOUT MY LAST JOB AND WHY	EVIDENCE	NEGATIVE THINGS ABOUT MY LAST JOB AND WHY
Tasks or activities			
Skills			
Relationships			
Results			

Now that you have a list of things that you enjoy about your job and an indication of what you don't enjoy and why, you can start to research other jobs and organisations that could offer you positive things. You have also taken the first step towards being able to explain to an interviewer what you can do, what skills you have to offer, why you like a task and what you are looking for in your next role.

■ Describing what I'm good at and enjoy doing

The job search process is time consuming, sometimes daunting and occasionally intimidating. If you have no idea of where you want to go or how you arrived at your current start point, then it will always be fruitless. You will end up with a job eventually, even during times of high unemployment but it will be just that: a stopgap job that earns you some money but does not contribute to your career development or fulfilment. It might even turn into your nightmare job as described on the right hand side of the previous grid. In order to nail the right job that develops your skills, experiences and career, you need to have a deep understanding of who you are, what you want from your next job and how it will connect to the rest of your career. You must also understand clearly what you have to offer your next employer and which employer might have the ideal job that has the right mix of demands for you.

The next exercise helps you to build on your list of skills, competences and achievements that you started in Exercise 1. Effectively, I'm giving you a 'map' for you to collect all your thoughts about what you are good at and what you enjoy, to help you focus on what sort of work is right for you. If you are comfortable with the concept of mind maps, then draw one out on a blank sheet of paper. If the phrase 'mind map' means nothing to you, then try using the WOW factor visualisation below. All you have to do is put examples of the categories asked for into the right section of the map for you. Here's where you get to use the wallpaper! *(See over page.)*

The 'wallpaper technique'

This WOW map asks you to describe what you're really good at and enjoy doing at work. Anything that you do well gets scribbled in the outside circle. Stuff that you know you do **very** well, probably better than most of your colleagues gets listed in the middle circle and in the inside circle you list everything that you do that makes your boss say, "Wow!" There is no place anywhere on this map for you to write stuff you do not feel confident about or do not enjoy.

Roll out about 60 centimetres of the wallpaper, (more if you have big writing), turn it over to the blank side, draw out your circles and write up the headings opposite. Use a set of sticky notes to write up each example. The sticky notes are useful for changing your mind: you can easily move a note if you decide to change its position in the WOW map.

> *"The best careers advice to give to the young is: find out what you like doing best and get someone to pay you for doing it."* KATHERINE WHITEHORN, *The Observer* journalist

Now is not the time to be shy. Often when I introduce this exercise to people they find it difficult to get going. We are not used to identifying clearly what we are good at and many people find it embarrassing. If you are struggling on this one, then refer back to your list of competences in Exercise 1 to remind yourself of what you know you can do well. The secret of this exercise is to focus on what we really do well **and** enjoy doing. The rest of your career is at stake here; this exercise identifies the key skills that you have to offer your next employer. You will shine when you present this at interview because you have clearly defined that this is what you enjoy doing. You are the only person who can put the activities into the right circle; this exercise often works better without a friend/relative/colleague adding their opinion.

EXERCISE 4: The WOW map – what I'm good at and enjoy doing

Example

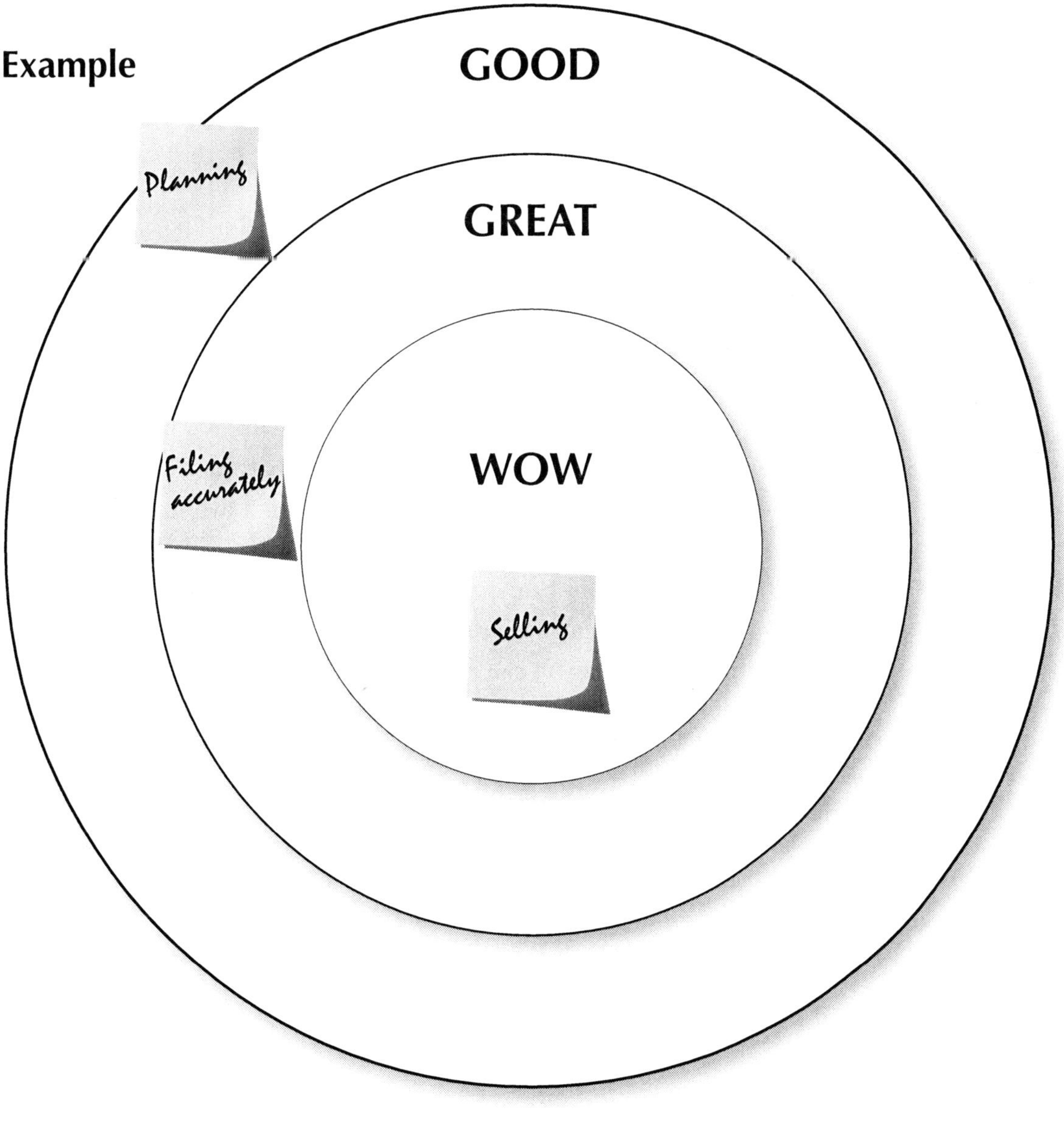

Now that you have clarified what you like doing at work and what you are good at, you will be able to use this map as the base for your CV descriptions. You will be more confident in describing to a recruiter the successful aspects of your career simply because you have now accurately defined and rehearsed them. If a particular job advert or potential opportunity crops up, you will be able to tune into what the recruiter is asking for quickly and match it up with what you have to offer.

■ What are you looking for?

The next part of the process is to be clear about what you are looking for. Many jobseekers I work with start out a little hazy about precisely what they are looking for – frequently people are clearer about what they don't want. My approach to jobseeking is to challenge you to search out the right job that will give you long-term career development and personal satisfaction.

"Take care to get what you like or you will be forced to like what you get."

GEORGE BERNARD SHAW,
20th century Irish playwright and co-founder of the London School of Economics

What do you want and need from your next job? This is a huge question but one that is very simple to answer. Remember that 'want' and 'need' often have different meanings. For example I may ***want*** a two seat soft-top sports car in which I could bowl along the road enjoying the wind in my hair, singing along loudly to my favourite music. What I actually ***need*** is a set of the most reliable and cost-effective wheels I can afford with enough space to fit several rapidly growing teenagers, two very scruffy dogs and a big enough boot to manage the family camping holiday. My soft-top sports car becomes a longer-term spending ambition. Your ideal job may be three or even more jobs away in your career. To reach your ideal job you need to understand which jobs will be the right ones for your interim steps along the route. This exercise is all about getting the balance right between where you're starting from now and what your next job will give you. You cannot begin to assess what your next step is if you don't know where you want to go.

After you have completed the next exercise, called 'Wants and Needs', you will be able to describe your ideal job, and identify the most likely places for you to start looking for it. You'll also be able to see how far away from it you are now and consequently you'll be able to determine your interim job steps. To get you started, I have found that the following two headings are most useful to help jobseekers consider all of what they want and what they need:

- **Material things**
- **Personal/social/emotional needs**

Material things

This expression covers all the tangible benefits of any job. These include salary and pension, which are the most common financial benefits that are on offer. Most jobseekers do not look far beyond these two parts of a jobs package. However, potentially there is also a long list of smaller benefits that may make a big difference to you when considering what your ideal job is, such as bonuses, incentive/commission schemes, contribution to childcare costs or travel costs, health insurance, company car, subsidised food, accommodation, allowances for clothing or equipment you provide, discount schemes, share save schemes, opportunities for flexible working, opportunities to progress through pay bands, payment of professional fees or licences and extra payment for learning new skills. Just in case you were wondering, there is no job on earth that offers all of these benefits! I'm just trying to widen your expectations of the total benefits package that may be on offer.

The issue you need to be clear about at the start of your job search is the distinction between what you want and what you need and where want and need overlap. If you are clear from the start about which bits of any particular benefits package are the most important to you, when you receive a job offer, you will be able to quickly assess precisely how closely it matches what you want and therefore be in a strong position to negotiate something slightly different if you want to.

EXERCISE 5: Clarifying material wants and needs

POTENTIAL MONETARY BENEFIT	THIS IS IMPORTANT TO ME BECAUSE:
Salary	
Pension	
Bonus scheme	
Company car	
Discount scheme	
Equipment/clothing allowances	
Flexible working hours	
Health insurance	
Help with childcare costs	
Help with travel costs	
Incentive/commission	
Payment for new skills/training or qualifications	
Professional membership fees/ licenses paid	
Regular progression through pay bands	
Share scheme	
Subsidised food/ accommodation	

Personal/Social/Emotional

This heading covers what is important to you about the way you work and the non-financial benefits that you gain from paid employment. You have probably heard of the phrase 'work-life balance' and this is part of what I am asking you to define for yourself here. Most people use the phrase to describe the tension between too-heavy demands from paid employment and the rest of your family and social life. Remember that boredom and lack of challenge are just as stressful as dealing with too much work and the key word to focus on here is 'balance'. Exercises 2 and 3 are a good start point for this topic. I'm now asking you to start exploring what you would like from your ideal job in terms of personal, social and emotional needs.

There is an old fashioned word that might be helpful here: 'vocation'. If someone describes their paid employment as a vocation, then it is often seen as having fewer of the material benefits as described in Exercise 5 but provides mental and/ or emotional fulfilment for the job holder in the sense of delivering a great service. One person's stimulating vocation could be the next person's extremely boring job. Clearly you are the only person who can define 'stimulating' and 'boring', so again there is no wrong answer to what you write in this exercise.

> *"Good hours, excellent pay, fun place to work, paid training, mean boss. Oh well, four out of five isn't bad."*
>
> 'Help wanted' advertisement in American national paper

A vital part of this activity is the set of three prompt sentences that ask you to describe in a lot of detail how you see your future ideal job in what you are:

- doing,
- feeling and
- saying as you carry out this job.

A lot of jobseekers I work with find these questions very powerful for clarifying precisely what they are looking for. Research on visualisation shows that the greater the detail that goes into your visualisation of your ideal state, then the more likely it is that you will reach that state.

An important part of your reflections here must be about your employment status. This is whether you want to be employed, self-employed (as a self starter or through a franchise route), freelance or agency worker. All of these categories of employment can also be undertaken as full or part-time, temporary or permanent. Higher up the professional ladder, temporary jobs are described as 'interim appointments'. Some occupations, for example IT technicians, hairdressers and tree surgeons, are usually employed on a contract or freelance basis, rarely as direct employees. There are clear legal distinctions between these types of employment contracts and you should check which is right for you at this point in your career and personal life.

Historically, both employees and recruiters may have looked down their noses a bit at temporary or contract work – but no longer. Some professions now favour people who have worked in a series of temporary posts to widen their experience and recruiters may value breadth of experience over stability of employment. Whatever your experience of employment has been so far, I would advise you not to rule out a particular post just because it will change your employment status. The entire purpose of this activity is for you to be in control of your own criteria about what type of work makes your ideal job.

Another issue to consider here is the needs of any dependents or your wider family. For example, you may be clear that your next job simply has to be part time, or that you can only afford to spend a maximum of 20 minutes travelling. Some of you may be happy to consider working in a different country, which is just as valid a decision as choosing to work no further than 20 minutes from home. An additional point to make about commuting is that you should always measure it in time rather than distance, regardless of how you propose to travel to work. The direct cost plus time invested in commuting is always a more accurate picture of the toll it takes on your physical, mental and emotional reserves than merely measuring the distance travelled. Twenty miles notoriously takes very different times to travel, depending on the mode of transport and where those miles are in Britain.

The focused jobseeker ensures that they have actively considered all possible personal, social and emotional aspects of their total job options and then rules out everything that does not match their criteria. Instantly their time then spent jobseeking is put to much better use. It is a sad, but true, fact that recruiters commonly see job offers turned down by strong candidates, who only realise once they have the job offer in their hand that they don't want to disturb the rest of the family by moving 200 miles. Save time for yourself and everyone else involved in recruiting by having a go at the following activity.

Most people find it helpful to complete it on their own first, then discuss the results with key family members and then adjust the answers if necessary. Consequently, I'd recommend using a pencil. If you need more space, then roll out some more wallpaper.

EXERCISE 6: Clarifying personal, social and emotional needs

KEY PERSONAL, SOCIAL AND EMOTIONAL NEEDS FROM MY IDEAL NEXT JOB	THIS IS IMPORTANT TO ME BECAUSE:
Boredom means for me . . .	
Distance I am prepared to travel to work	
Good development opportunities mean . . .	
Hours of work needed	
I am prepared to relocate as far as . . .	
Important values to apply at work are . . .	

This exercise is continued on following page

KEY PERSONAL, SOCIAL AND EMOTIONAL NEEDS FROM MY IDEAL NEXT JOB	THIS IS IMPORTANT TO ME BECAUSE:
Industries I must work for or must avoid on moral grounds	
In my ideal job, I am doing . . .	
In my ideal job, I am feeling . . .	
In my ideal job I am saying. . .	
Job satisfaction means for me. . .	
My employment status should be. . .	
Scale/size of organisation needed. . .	
Tasks I must be engaged in. . .	
The right scale of challenge for me is. . .	
Work/life balance means for me. . .	

■ Putting it all together

So by this point, you have given a great deal of thought to your material, personal, social and emotional needs for your next job. The next step is to define the most important criteria for your long-term ideal job, which you may now have realised, is several roles away. This is the role that you have identified as your ultimate target. Especially when the jobs market is tough, it is helpful for you to be clear about what your ideal job looks like. Try putting together the work from the last three exercises to identify what your ideal job looks like and how close you are already to fulfilling it.

Sometimes, completing this next activity demonstrates for jobseekers that actually they are now in their ideal job. Why you may not have noticed this is a different question but should lead you into some reflection about what small changes you could make to change how you feel about work.

Reflect on all your evidence from the last three exercises and draw out another WOW map on the next stretch of wallpaper. This one, laid out in the same way as the first one, asks you to identify and rank all the things that would make your ideal job a WOW one and working out from the central circle, down to just a good job. If you think you are running out of room, another way to tackle this brainstorming is to arrange the sticky notes on the wall in concentric circles. If it suits your reflecting style, then choose different colours to colour code your ideas.

EXERCISE 7: My 2nd WOW map – what will make my next job my ideal job

Example

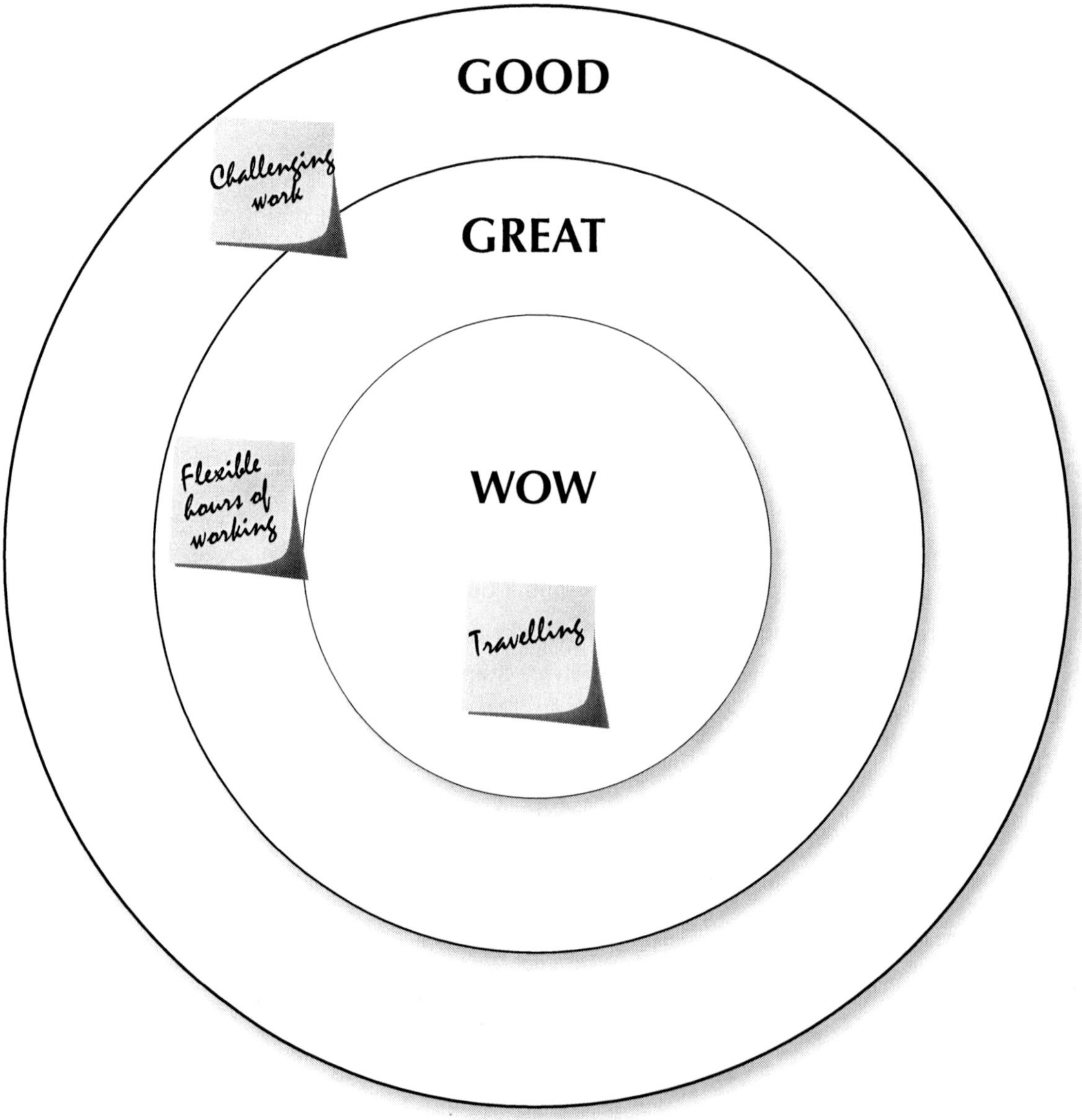

Your 'Meeting Prince Charles Speech'

Just imagine that at your current or last workplace, a member of the Royal Family arrives on tour. If you are a committed republican, then simply visualise your favourite left-wing politician or hero. Any VIP visit has extremely tight deadlines and there are always a lot of hands to shake. I have it on good authority (from someone who used to help plan such events) that members of the Royal Family are genuinely interested in each individual's response to their eternal question: "So what do you do then?" At that point they expect a clear, interesting and succinct reply that describes what that person contributes to the organisation that they are visiting. They then have to move on swiftly to the next handshake. Just like royal interviewees, every jobseeker has to be able to present their key talents and what they are looking for very quickly and clearly.

There is a short proverb that is helpful to remember here:

"You only get one chance to make a first impression."

All you have to do is generate your own sentence, or a maximum of two sentences that summarise who you are, what you have to offer and what you are looking for. I always suggest starting in front of the bathroom mirror and please do say the words out loud to check how they sound when coming from you. This exercise has proved an astonishing confidence boost for so many jobseekers I have worked with.

As you work through more of this book, you will come back to this speech and polish it further as more of your job search becomes clear to you. Try following the model below and insert the words that make sense for you.

"Hello, I'm Dave Smith and I've recently been made redundant from a team leader role in retail computer support. I'm currently looking for work in computing support in the service sector as I have a lot of relevant technical experience and strong team motivational skills to offer."

As you develop more clarity about what you're seeking, you can refine your examples and start tailoring them to the audience that you are meeting. This statement is useful to get you started at network meetings (more on networking on page 36 in Chapter 2), interview practice and in any social occasion where it would be helpful to alert the people you meet that you are an active jobseeker. The principles of creating your 'Meeting Prince Charles Speech' are:

1 Keep it brief.

2 Make the wording your own; it has to sound natural and comfortable in your own voice.

3 Consequently, practise out loud. Testing it out on your nearest and dearest is optional and depends on how highly you value their experience and opinion.

4 Summarise for the listener who you are, the most significant talent you have that can add value to a future employer and the sort of role or industry you are looking for.

5 Anticipate the response depending on the situation. So long as you are ready for a range of potential responses, you will find yourself having a short conversation with a stranger about the most fascinating topic on the planet: you and your many talents.

Let's summarise at this point what you have discovered about yourself, your talents and your preferences for using them in work:

- ***You have a list of what you are good at and how it overlaps with what you enjoy.***
- ***You have a feel for tasks, experiences and skills that you would like to develop further or use more of in future work.***
- ***You know which experiences you would like to leave behind and, most importantly, why.***
- ***You can describe with precision what you want and need from your next job, both materially and emotionally.***
- ***You can summarise for a stranger your core offer for a future employer and a direction for your job search.***
- ***You can describe clearly for yourself what your ideal job looks, feels and sounds like and have an idea about how close you are to that job currently.***

Now you are ready to start looking for it.

CHAPTER

2

Finding the right job

… and ensuring your research is time- and cost-effective

By the end of this chapter, you will be able to:

- ***Identify and use your personal networks to support your job search.***
- ***Plan and implement a professional and appropriate direct approach to target organisations through face-to-face meetings, phone calls or emails.***
- ***Identify potential job vacancies, including unadvertised ones.***
- ***Maximise your time spent on internet research.***
- ***Make recruitment agencies' websites work hard for you.***
- ***Ensure that you maximise your accessibility to recruiters.***
- ***Test your job search progress against your long-term career goals.***
- ***Target the right organisations for you.***

■ Tracking down the right opportunities

How did you find your last/current job? It was probably through one of the following sources:

1 Direct advert (organisational website, national/regional newspaper, trade press, radio)
2 Recruitment agency or Jobcentre
3 Word of mouth/Networking to identify unadvertised vacancies
4 Direct approach (by phone, email/letter)
5 Self-employment

The first two routes are often referred to as the 'visible' job market and the next two as the 'hidden' job market. Self-employment is always another option for you: it also requires a huge amount of research to clarify your business idea and get support from the bank. Estimates vary about how many jobs are in each category; my recruitment experience suggests that it varies widely according to industry. Let's sort out some facts from the myths.

Today, as you read this book, there are tens of thousands of vacancies in the total national labour market, some of which haven't yet even been identified by the managers of the missing workers. No one can measure precisely how many, although the government does attempt to in its regular survey of employment issues. They vary tremendously in situation, geography, scope, employment status, hours and all the other categories that you considered in your exercises in Chapter 1 to define your ideal job. The official vacancy figures do not cover potential self-employment options. Best estimates suggest that of all these potential vacancies for you, as many as 70 per cent could be unadvertised, i.e. in the 'hidden' market.

If you have worked largely in the public sector, that figure may come as a surprise to you. If you have worked largely in the private sector, you may be surprised to learn that all public sector employers have a duty under the Equality Act 2010 to promote equality of opportunity by encouraging historically disadvantaged groups to participate more in public life. This is usually interpreted as an expectation to advertise every vacancy. This does not mean a requirement for a full paper advertisement; commonly the most cost-effective solution for public sector employers is to advertise vacancies on their websites. Even in localities where unemployment rates are high and large employers are not recruiting, there will still be work to do; your task is to find that work and assess how closely it matches what you want and need. Your key learning here then is that work is out there and thorough research will unearth it.

The core disadvantage of the hidden labour market is clearly that a lot of time and energy has to be put into uncovering it. Your big advantage is that when you have unearthed a potential vacancy that suits you, you have no or virtually nil competition and you have already impressed the potential employer with your qualities of perseverance and commitment. If employers are willing to take the time to read the CV of a candidate who approaches them directly – even if the job isn't the best fit, or the current budget means that it cannot go ahead for another six months – your details may be filed. I have recruited people out of the 'promising' drawer of recent applicants. The 'promising' drawer includes all sorts of people who didn't quite make the grade at the last interview, or we thought were perhaps not quite right for the job they did apply for but might be a better fit in a different job, plus all the strong direct approaches we had been sent recently. 'Recently' probably means within about the last six months; it's not worth the employer keeping CVs much longer than that as the applicants' circumstances will probably have moved on. The big advantage to the employer of dipping into their 'promising' file is, of course, to save the costs of advertising. Please note however, that if the 'promising' drawer does not come up with any potential candidates, then the job will swiftly move into the visible market.

> *"A goal without a plan is just a wish."*
>
> ANTOINE DE SAINT EXUPERY, Author and pilot

CASE STUDY

Direct approaches pay off

I am only one of many jobseekers who have landed a job offer through the direct approach method. Once upon a time, I responded to a trade press job advertisement and secured an interview with a national retailer. I wasn't offered the post, but had some very positive feedback and my CV was clearly held in the 'promising' drawer. Several months later, I read a report about the retailer in the financial press and decided to approach them again.

Effectively, I had kept up my research on my target organisation. They had just decided to expand a different department, one which they felt my experience matched better than my original application. Consequently, I had another interview for a different job with the same organisation against very little competition. Three of us out of their 'promising' drawer were offered jobs in the expanding department with no direct recruitment costs to the company.

How to reveal the 'hidden' jobs market

The most useful key to start unlocking the hidden market is through networking. This does not mean that you should invite yourself to every public meeting in your region and demand to know from everyone you meet if they know of a job going in their organisation. Job search networking requires more subtle conversations and you cannot expect immediate responses. Recently, politicians have provoked a debate about young people from more privileged backgrounds networking their way into competitive, unpaid or poorly paid entry roles. Historically, jobs of all kinds in all industries have for many generations been offered to people already known within the business, simply because the known was safer for the employer than the unknown. The modern labour market is now far more sophisticated and regulated to ensure better equality of opportunity to all applicants. (On page 198 is a brief guide to legislation that protects job applicants from discrimination during recruitment.)

More effective than the threat of legislation to employers and fines for non-compliance, is the cost of making the wrong recruitment decision. Every recruiter has one simple aim: to ensure that they find the best possible candidate for the job. Anything less than that results in poor performance by the wrong jobholder and terrifying costs for the employer to remedy the situation later. I cannot stress too much the overlap of interest that you have with any recruiter that you meet: you want to find the right job for you, and they want to find the right candidate for their vacancy. A successful result for both parties means that the right person performs well in the right role. If you find yourself rejected from an application, it is for a sound reason and every professional recruiter will be comfortable about giving you feedback about how you did not match up to what they were looking for.

Your jobseeking task is to present clearly how well you match up to what the employer is looking for. Having completed the activities in Chapter 1, you now have a sound understanding of what you have to offer and an idea of which sort of employers are most likely to be looking for it. Networking is a vital and legitimate process to research your target industries and organisations; build up your own profile and credibility;

develop your knowledge, skills and understanding; enable you to help someone else in the industry; expand your contacts; and **incidentally** provides a good source of information about the potential for unadvertised job vacancies. Everyone you know is a potential contact for offering advice and support in your job search. Let's start listing who you know.

"... those who learn to network successfully will soon be as highly prized in the job market as those with more traditional 'hard' skills and qualifications. And the... research is mounting that connections and the exchange of ideas are much more likely to yield better job prospects."

JULIA HOBSBAWM, Visiting Professor in Networking, London's Cass Business School

CASE STUDY

Networking works

Perhaps the best story I have come across about the power of networking is set at a school swimming gala. Barry had been made redundant from a water supplier, as an Operations Manager leading emergency repair teams. His research, using the activities you have covered in Chapter 1, had led him to the conclusion that he now wanted a job with less managerial responsibility and closer to the sort of 'hands on' work that he had enjoyed at the beginning of his career. Bearing in mind the power of networking, he saw the value of telling everyone he met that he was looking for this sort of work.

He was watching his daughter race in a school swimming gala and struck up conversation with the mother sitting next to him. Her husband ran a central heating installation and maintenance company and was desperate for skilled plumbing engineers. You can guess the end of the story. Barry nailed himself the right job because he was happy to discuss his job search plans with a complete stranger.

The page opposite is a blank network map for you to complete. Simply write down the names of everyone you know who may have information about potential vacancies in the industries that you want to target.

Draw lines to represent how you know them and how they connect through your friends. Check again the list above of all potential objectives you could have for networking and you will quickly see that just about everyone you know may be able to give you some advice, or the name of someone else who may be able to help you in your job search.

If you are still struggling to identify all those people who could help, then use one of the following checklists. The same individual will probably appear in several categories, which doesn't matter.

What you need to do here is think as widely as possible about every daily human contact you have.

- relatives
- friends
- the family Christmas card list
- current work colleagues (some discretion may be needed here)
- past work colleagues
- neighbours
- your postman/woman (I have another story about a conversation with a chatty postman who alerted a jobseeker to the fact that a company at the other end of the post round was looking for more staff.)
- your local community of worship
- current/past fellow students
- every new person you meet at a social event
- your local branch of the relevant professional organisation or membership group
- every member of any hobby, sport or personal interest group you attend
- the school gate community if you are regularly collecting younger children from school
- online friends

For an alternative list, see page 40

EXERCISE 1: Identifying all possible contacts

My network map

There is an alternative way of categorising this list – try placing their names under these headings:

- People (including current and past customers) who will sing your praises (potential referees).
- People who could give you productive and honest feedback on your job search objectives or your CV.
- People who could help you increase your professional visibility.
- People who know how to reach others who you may find helpful.
- People who will challenge you to grow as a person.
- People who could act as a mentor/guide to help you make key decisions in your job search plan.
- People with specific technical/industry or professional knowledge that will help you learn more about your target roles.
- People with useful information (potentially a huge group).
- Anyone who might have an unused roll of wallpaper in a cupboard (i.e. any other category that you care to name!).

There is an urban myth about everyone being connected to the Queen by only six degrees of separation, i.e. we all know someone who knows someone, who knows someone, who knows someone, who knows someone who has met the Queen. I have no idea if those statistics really work across a population of 62 million with a very long serving head of state. It is a neat demonstration of how the more interconnected you are, the more options you have for enabling an introduction to someone in your target industry who may be able to give you advice about career development, or organisations which may have some hidden vacancies.

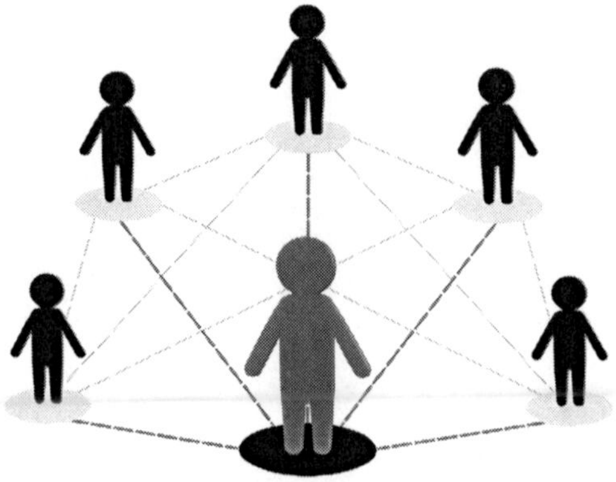

Some golden rules for networking

Whoever you meet under whatever circumstances when it is appropriate to talk about your job search aims, there are some general principles about networking behaviour that will in the long run make it a more effective process for you and all the people you meet. The core principle of networking is that it is a life-long career sustainer and should continue to be practised once you are settled in a new job. You never know when someone who has offered you advice/assistance may request the same from you in the future. Essentially, the successful jobseeker simply focuses a natural process of relationship building that we all do instinctively to a greater or lesser degree to oil the wheels of daily life. It is always a good idea to participate in online networking, through trade or professional communities, but there is no substitute in terms of building relationships for meeting people face to face and professional networking is all about building relationships. There is more information on managing online networks on page 57.

Dos of networking

- Practise your 'Meeting Prince Charles Speech' to get it fluent *(see Chapter 1 page 31)*.
- Ask how you might be able to help people.
- Always say thank you, whatever the outcome of the conversation.
- Research beforehand what possible information anyone in the room may have.
- Be organised with your contact details to hand.
- Be clear in what you are asking for.
- Keep the conversation/meeting brief.
- At a formal networking meeting, move round as many people in the room as you can.
- Leave a positive impression.
- Generate a specific objective for following up any conversation.
- Follow up swiftly; within at least one week.
- Respond to rejection politely and positively.
- Keep organised records of contact details; you may want to go back to someone months later.

Don'ts of networking

- Ask if people have a job for you.
- Hog one person's time.
- Overwhelm anyone with the details of your job search.
- Present yourself vaguely or negatively.

Potential opportunities to network

- Local business groups/chambers of commerce.
- Local/regional meetings of professional associations.
- Jobs fairs.
- Trade exhibitions.
- Online through professional/trade networks.
- Social events (only when it is appropriate).

Making contacts and direct approaches through email and phone

In order to maximise your networking time, you need to research your best prospects for directly approaching your target organisations and individuals. Internet research will only get you so far; at some point you need to speak to a human being. You may secure the correct name, job title or even email address of the person you would like to speak to, but everyone in the modern workplace is busy and emails can be easily ignored. A key prize for you to discover is the phone number of your target person and just to get that requires patience, organisation and a little bit of cheek, always politely packaged.

Structure for networking/researching through email and phone

All communication to gather information or establish a relationship through any media should be kept brief and clear. Before you pick up the phone or start typing, make sure that you are well organised: have all your research on this organisation or person to hand and consider whether this is a good time for them. Every industry has its peak times of day or year: for example, don't try to contact accountants in late March, schools in late December or July, or retailers in the second half of the working week.

Your 'Meeting Prince Charles Speech' will be a helpful springboard for a focused phone conversation and your confidence will be boosted by rehearsing what you want to say. Have a look at the preparing for interview guidance in Chapter 4 on page 113 for some more ideas about managing any nerves you may have about phoning a complete stranger and asking for help. When emailing, proofread your final product at least three times before pressing 'send'. This is your first chance to make a favourable impression in an organisation, so make sure that all your facts and spellings are correct. If you are a keen texter, please don't even consider using 'text speak 'in an email; it is simply inappropriate outside text messages. Whether you are emailing or phoning, you will stand a much better chance of the message being paid attention to if you address it directly to a name rather than just a job title.

The structure of any email or phone approach should be:

1 Introduction; understand who I am and how I reached them

For example:

> *Hello, my name is . . . and I was given your name by . . . who worked with you on Project X. I'm currently researching a career move into your industry and wondered if you have a few moments to talk about what you see as the core skills for entering your business.*

At the very beginning, the listener/reader must instantly understand who you are, how you have reached them and what you are asking for. You need to arouse some interest in them to read or listen further to you. Very few people can resist a politely phrased, genuine request to share their expertise, as it is a flattering question.

TIP

Practice makes perfect

As you close your first proactive networking call, you will feel immensely positive. You have taken control of your job search and introduced yourself to a stranger. Your next call will be significantly easier.

2 Specify your request for specific information

For example:

> *I'd like to emphasise that I'm simply asking for a little career advice about what recruiters are looking for in your industry and if you could clarify entry expectations across the industry. I'm not asking whether your company has any current vacancies.*

Reassurance is the key word here; you must quickly make it clear what you're not going to do, i.e. embarrass them by asking for a job. When phoning, they need to know that they won't be talking for very long. When emailing, they need to quickly read your list of specific questions, absolute maximum to ask in one email should be three. If you want to know more, then ask again later, once your relationship has developed further.

3 Engage interest in your background

For example:

> *My background is in industry Y; I have three years of management experience leading a team of five people in administration and my key skills lie in A and B. I'd be very interested in your view of how relevant you think that skills A and B are for your industry.*

By this point, you have engaged their interest and now have the opportunity to apply part of your polished 'Meeting Prince Charles Speech' here. This is your chance to impress on them that you have something to offer and are not merely a random telemarketer. If you are not ready now with your succinct description of what you have to offer, you will hear their interest rapidly fading away. On a poorly constructed research email, most people will have stopped reading by now if they do not think you have something to offer them in return for their time and expertise.

4 Next steps

For example:

> *If it is convenient for you, I would be very interested in holding a brief meeting with you next week to discuss entry points to your industry. Could you suggest a time that would be helpful to you please?*

Close the conversation or email with your specific request that will fulfil the objective of your message. Take responsibility for the next step but always state your request politely and clearly; they have to know that they remain in control of their busy diary.

Please note that the words above are a guide example, not a script. When you plan your direct approach or research calls and emails, make the words your own and make sure that they support what you have already discovered in your research to date. Opposite is a blank copy of a plan for a direct approach phone call or email. Photocopy the blank pages and/or use pencil for drafting your own plan for your next networking call or email. When phoning, you clearly need to anticipate their responses, so there are spaces on the page for you to jot down some suggestions and remind yourself that you are planning a conversation, not a monologue.

Be prepared for rejections; it would be astonishing if you always reached the right person at exactly the right time for them. Use objections as an opportunity to learn and still repeat the words, "Thank you for your time". Don't take the rejection personally; you are trying to speak to or email busy people and irritating a potential contact creates much more damage for your long-term job search aims than losing the opportunity for one meeting.

EXERCISE 2: Plan for a direct approach phone call or email

My overall objective for this message is to:

(See the bottom of page 36 and the top of page 48 for potential objectives.)

(a) Introduction: *Understand who I am, how I am connected and what I am looking for*

WHAT I SAY:

THEY MIGHT SAY:

This exercise is continued on following page

(b) Specific request: *Clear, brief, reassuring and polite*

WHAT I SAY:

THEY MIGHT SAY:

(c) Engage their interest: *Show what I have to offer*

WHAT I SAY:

THEY MIGHT SAY:

(d) Next steps: *Courteously take the responsibility for action. Always close with a thank you*

WHAT I SAY:

THEY MIGHT SAY:

To summarise then; the purpose of calling or emailing around your networking contacts could be any one or a combination of the following objectives:

- Reinforce and spread your jobseeking message.
- Deepen your understanding of a particular job market or technical knowledge to support an application you are currently making.
- Research key people who may be able to extend your network.
- Ask for advice or feedback on your job search to date.
- Identify potential opportunities for vacancies.

Essentially these are the same objectives as for face-to-face networking, discussed earlier at the bottom of page 36. The same golden rules apply about approaching strangers politely and with a clear intention.

If you are lucky enough to secure a brief formal meeting with a key contact, then plan for this in the same manner as you would for a formal interview *(see Chapter 4, page 111)*. You never know how influential that meeting could be or where it could lead you. Even if there are no opportunities in the home organisation of the person you meet, through his or her networks, your details may get passed on to another organisation and the power of making a good impression is that you will then have a personal recommendation attached to your name.

■ Making the most out of time spent researching on the internet

The global internet is a fantastic tool for the jobseeker, enabling you to research organisations, individuals, industries, qualification routes, recruitment agencies, business trends and truly global markets for those considering emigration. Effectively most, but crucially not all, of what you need to know as a jobseeker can be found online. It is also the biggest time waster for those who don't know what they are looking for or how to make the most of this resource. I've worked with jobseekers of all ages who have got lost online; mesmerised by too much information, they allowed their job search to become paralysed. Let's go back to basics.

The internet has transformed recruitment over the last decade, changing processes and approaches to recruitment in every industry. Depending on your industry experience and the length of time since you were last in the job market, you may be a little unclear about how to make the most of this crucial jobseeking tool. You may be of an age group that takes it for granted that your job search starts online but you might be missing out on opportunities for face-to-face research. Essentially, using the internet for job search has two crucial applications:

- as a research tool for all potential opportunities, organisational and industry information
- as a showcase for your talents, skills and abilities

You need to stay in control of both of these processes in order to maximise your time spent online. I will not provide for you a list of helpful websites. It would be already out of date by the time you have finished reading this book. I can offer my experience of online trends that have current relevance to recruitment, focusing on the UK labour market. By applying the following guidelines, you can make sure that you are genuinely using the internet to your best advantage and not wasting time.

Some of the most organised – and consequently successful – jobseekers I work with are those who do not have their own direct internet connection and are therefore reliant on libraries and internet cafés for online access. When you have to pay directly in hourly rates for your web research, it immediately focuses the mind on your daily objectives for information gathering. I'd recommend always keeping an eye on the time you spend online and before pressing the on button, writing down a list of what you need to find out today and reviewing it on an hourly basis. Wherever and however you are using the web, please make sure you have paper, pencil and memory stick to hand to keep on top of your notes.

Incidentally, if you only have online access through libraries or internet cafés, then you get far more for your money from libraries. In my experience, even the coffee tastes better in a library too. Librarians are the undiscovered heroes of any job search campaign. They do this job because they get a kick out of helping people discover stuff. They will probably have advice on a local course for you to become more confident online. They know a lot about the current helpful websites for jobseekers and many develop expertise in particular careers, so a brief conversation with them will save you days of wandering about online. They even have access to some old-fashioned tools called books and journals and can show you the most helpful reference and trade publications to support your research. Currently, librarians are having a tough time and deserve all the support we can give them. If you develop a relationship with your friendly local librarian and tell them the sorts of roles or industries you are interested in, they will be delighted to save you time.

A few things to avoid when researching online

- **Distractions:** turn off your email alert noises or simply use willpower and do not open incoming emails until you have achieved your research targets.
- **Wikipedia** – it's largely compiled by enthusiastic amateurs. Consider who in society has most time on their hands to indulge in unpaid 'factual' writing and ponder where they may be sourcing their information. I appreciate that it might get you started on a profitable line of research, but leave it behind quickly and concentrate on more reputable sources.
- **Relying on the back button** to find a page you read 15 minutes and 11 sites ago. If a page takes your fancy while you want to move onto another topic or use a link, just pause briefly to tag the interesting page onto your favourites bar/bookmark and you will be able to find it again quickly. At the end of any research session, briefly review and tidy up that favourites list, just to keep it manageable.

> *"Data, data everywhere but never time to think."*
> PROFESSOR SONIA LIVINGSTONE, London School of Economics

Once you have your daily research targets ready, where can you go online to get the most from every site you visit? All of the following categories will be helpful to you at some point in your job search:

Organisational websites

Virtually every organisation, whether they have current vacancies or not, has an online presence. The amount of public information available varies tremendously according to the size and context of the organisation but, at minimum, you should be able to find a contact number or email to pursue further enquiries. In the current climate, many organisations advertise any vacancies they have on their websites and tend not to spend advertising money outside their own site unless they are seeking pretty specialised skills, large numbers or are in the public sector. An organisation's website is a good start point to researching how it might feel to work for that particular organisation, but is no substitute for managing to speak directly to someone who currently works there. Essentially many modern recruitment processes are designed to start online and actively filter out a large number of applicants to provide a shortlist for interview. You can find more information on managing online applications in Chapters 3, page 86 and 5, page 166. If your target organisation has any sort of newsletter or marketing blog to sign up for, then sign up for it to keep in touch with them.

You might have noticed recently the increasing use of smartphone codes by larger organisations. A paper or magazine advertisement of job opportunities or products includes a small smartphone code for you to scan and be linked directly to a key page on the organisation's website, which may or may not be accessible through any other route. It is a cost- and time-effective way of monitoring which advertising routes attract which candidates or customers. Never scan the advert on an impulse without being prepared. The smartphone link might push you immediately into a timed, informal initial screening application. There is more support on preparing for interviews in Chapter 4 from page 111.

Industry/professional/trade associations

Every trade has created its own professional organisation that safeguards everything from entry routes into a profession to mapping ethical and performance standards for each level of experience in that role. Again these associations vary tremendously in size and scope but all offer a great springboard into researching your target industry. These are particularly helpful if you are considering moving into a new industry. They may have a national or even regional office that includes a human being on the end of a phone for more detailed queries. Expect many of the larger associations to have restricted information that is only available to subscribing members. If it is really important to be able to see restricted areas of the site, then review your networks to see if you know someone in that organisation who may be prepared to sit with you at a computer using their entry passwords. Most national associations have regional groups managed on a volunteer basis which provide local networking meetings and further development opportunities with, for example, a guest speaker.

I include trades unions in this category of websites: the larger ones offer a wealth of information about specific industries, including, for example, indications of regional wage rates for different roles. Rarely will you see vacancies advertised through these sorts of sites, but their news sections are a great source of background industry information and could give you a clue to the key players in the business local to your target area.

Recruitment agencies and CV boards

There is more information on the vital art of managing recruitment agencies in Chapter 3 on page 101. The notes here focus on how to get the most out of a recruitment agency website. The key issue to remember is that although an internet search is likely to direct you onto the pages of a small number of giant, national agencies that cover all roles, you may well find it more productive to work with some of the smaller ones who focus on either local opportunities, or work with specific industries. You can probably quickly discover who the industry specific agencies are from the trade association websites. If you are already clear that you are targeting a particular industry, job role or geographical area, your time will be better spent turning up to those local offices in person or dealing directly with the industry expert recruiter. However, if you are still unclear about what you are looking for and want to test out your current CV, then the huge CV board sites are worth investigating.

The large-scale sites tend to make grand promises about how many employers are looking daily on their sites for your precise skill set. The most delicately phrased advice I can give you here is to treat these promises with a bucket of salt. Please note how recruitment agencies of all shapes and sizes make their money: when an employer takes on a candidate that they have found, they get a commission, which is a percentage of that job's salary. If you are inexperienced in using agencies, then your best plan is to take control of your relationship with them and regularly keep in touch with updates on your job search and to your CV. This is much harder to control in the giant CV boards that rely on churn and scale to place candidates. If you choose to use them, then you must be aware that you have placed your details into a huge pond of competitors and that's one possible route to finding a job, but the statistics are now stacked against you.

The home page of any agency will indicate whether they specialise in a particular industry, job role or location. If you decide to submit a CV to them, either in response to a specific advertisement, or just as a general application, be prepared for them to email you back an application form. There is more guidance on how to complete application forms in Chapter 3 on page 84. Whatever signing up processes they use (for example, some may ask for a maximum two page CV, or no CVs at all apart from their application form, or scans of driving licences or qualification certificates), please follow all the instructions carefully. If you get the initial application administration wrong, you will not endear yourself to the agency staff and will develop a reputation as someone who doesn't follow instructions well.

However you interact with them, make sure that very early on, you supplement your online application with a phone call to replicate the experience of regularly turning up at your local high street branch. Identify the name of a specific human being to whom you have addressed your CV: when connected, simply introduce yourself, check that they have received your CV and generate a networking conversation along the lines of the exercise you completed on page 45.

Other types of websites useful to jobseekers

Particularly if you are looking at routes to self-employment, then the following types of organisations will be helpful and each of these types of websites will also have further links to other relevant websites. I have not listed specific examples here as the internet dates so quickly, but the major search engines will come up with the goods if you type in general headings. Please remember the experience of the successful jobseekers who keep tabs on the time they spend online and the targets they set themselves for information gathering, in order not to waste time drifting online.

Chambers of Commerce websites offer a good source of local business based networking and have varying amounts of guidance on local self-employment opportunities and even vacancies. Much of this information is managed on a volunteer basis, and may not always be immaculately up to date but in terms of local knowledge and understanding of the key local trends affecting business of all kinds, this is a powerful network to tap into.

There is also a **national business support system** provided by the government under the Businesslink regional networks. There are a lot of online resources focused on business start up and development and regional face-to-face networking opportunities.

If you have decided to start up a business, then get some free resources out of the **big banks** by cruising around their websites for start up advice, then walk up and down your high street to identify in person the details of what they all have to offer. Some of the big banks have some pretty extensive resources to guide you through creating a business plan with useful pointers to all the things you will need to consider when starting from scratch. There is more detailed guidance on presenting a case for financing a business in Chapter 3 on page 104.

There are also **national franchise websites**, which are definitely the right place to start online if the idea of going into business on a tried-and-tested business plan appeals to you. Many franchises are offered for sale on these sites and again you will be able to tap into local or industry specific networks. You may be surprised to see the extent of nationally recognised businesses that are managed on a franchise basis. The modern franchise market has broken out of the retail and hospitality base that historically dominated franchise operations.

Government websites are extensive and not always obviously helpful to a job-seeker. If you want to spend long enough, you can find the answer to almost any query you have about a particular industry, but the organisation and presentation of most government websites is rarely user-friendly. Most government sites are established to serve the needs of experienced practitioners in specific fields rather than jobseekers less familiar with that field. Even the official portal to all government websites, www.direct.gov.uk, tends to connect you to a jargon-filled extract from a specialist website.

However, some can provide you with golden nuggets of information. This is truly an area where the professional help of a librarian will save you a lot of time, so long as you are clear about the sort of information you need. When it works, you can find out all sorts of things from government websites to support your jobseeking research: legal requirements for employment issues, industry-specific regulations, economic statistics and predictions for economic performance in your region/locality, planning issues, career and retraining resources, public sector vacancies, advice on benefits and grants of all kinds, access to all sorts of voluntary sector information, emigration advice and much more. It can send your research off into all sorts of unexpected directions, which is good for your jobseeking, so long as you are sticking to your online search objectives.

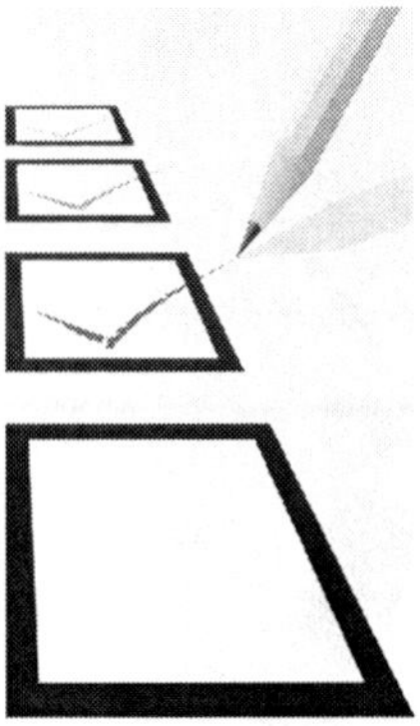

I hear mixed reports about **Jobcentres** from recent experiences of jobseekers I work with. To clarify one point; you do not have to be unemployed to access local vacancies on their website, which has become much more user friendly in recent times. Every vacancy is searchable from their site by location and job title. You may be looking for a quite specialised role, in which case their search facilities will be less useful to you but if nothing else, it will give you a feel for what local jobs are currently being advertised. The experience of getting support directly at your local Jobcentre office does appear to vary. Some offices are praised for their guidance of individuals, but I do hear that some jobseekers still feel as though staff are more concerned with ticking boxes than genuinely trying to support you in finding the right job for you. There is less direct commercial pressure on them than on recruitment agency staff to send you to the right job interview.

University and college websites also offer a wealth of information about qualification routes into all manner of job roles. Access to careers advice on these sites varies; some only allow current students entry, others are more generous with the amount of advice publicly available. Some colleges and universities have developed expertise in core industries, reinforcing historical local partnerships with employers in these industries and for some technical roles, they could be your best source of information about potential vacancies. As ever with web-based networking, if you discover the name and job role of a key person with relevant information for you, try to follow up an email approach with a face-to-face meeting to maximise your online research.

News sites are also a useful source of information: mobile access to the internet has speeded up response times to breaking news stories in a way that is clearly leaving the printed news media behind. On many news and information sites you can choose to subscribe to RSS feeds to alert you to breaking news on all kinds of issues. (RSS stands for really simple syndication, which means you give websites permission to directly alert you when they have updated information covering a specific topic.) They may provide you with a key news item that could prompt you to make a speculative application to a target organisation but beware the potential for distraction that these services offer. I will make a rare advert here for one specific website; www.bbc.co.uk has every possible work-related news item covered somewhere on its easily navigable, friendly site and the information provided can be trusted.

To summarise your key learning about using the internet for effective research:

- Effective jobseeking research means getting the accurate information you need as swiftly as possible.
- Set yourself some clear information targets and time targets for your daily research even when you are using your own equipment in the privacy of your own home.
- Keep organised records of sites visited. You could even set up your own rating system to categorise the ones that you find most helpful.
- Move as swiftly as you can from online to face-to-face networking. Less-experienced jobseekers can use the internet as a safe bolthole, you will view it as the springboard to reach possible job gatekeepers.
- When you hover over the 'Useful Links' section of any website, maintain that balance between an open mind and control of your time: pause to ensure that you understand what the new website is that you are clicking to and how it might add to your research. When in doubt, refer back to your objectives.

■ Control of your self-presentation online

Every internet user leaves their mark online that can be traced by those who are keen enough to do so. You may not always be aware of precisely what information is publicly viewable about you online but the responsible jobseeker ensures that they maximise all potential opportunities to present themselves in a positive light. As I write this, a national debate about the definition of personal privacy has recently been ignited by the behaviour of newspapers, which may yet deliver changes to legislation around privacy. A few years ago, a lively discussion about national security followed the revelation that the head of MI5 was viewable on a social networking site in his swimming trunks on a family holiday. You may have heard the urban myth of recruiters looking up candidates on social networking sites. Whatever your moral considerations about doing that, it does (rarely) happen and recruiters could only view what is publicly accessible. You should also be reassured that a recruiter would only devote precious time to researching a candidate online once they had reached the final stages of a shortlist or perhaps second interview.

Consequently, as you begin your job search, take time to review all publicly available information about you online. You do not of course have control about photos or other information involving you that friends or family also put online but you can always ask them to consider their own privacy settings. The national sniggering that followed the MI5 chief's swimming trunks photo could have easily been avoided if his wife had adjusted her privacy settings to allow only friends and family to access the photo. Unless you are considering a career in international espionage, recruiters can only view what you allow them to on your social networking sites.

Of far more use to the keen jobseeker than social networking sites are professional or industry-related ones. Every job role, profession or even locality has such networks that you need to be aware of once you have identified your target industries. They work on much the same principles as social networking but the language and presentation of information is of course oriented to professional networking needs. There is one current market leader that operates internationally and has numerous subgroups according to interests, location and industry but as ever in the online world, this dominance may change rapidly. They are currently virtually all free to join and make their money by advertising.

Creating a professional presence online and beginning to build your connections is a vital part of your jobseeker profile. You can invite others to join your network and ask for recommendations. There are various management tools to enable you to organise all those networking conversations online in the same way that you practised face-to-face networking in Exercise 2. These networks are also intended to support established jobholders, so for all currently employed jobseekers, this is also a test of your diplomacy and discretion. An unemployed jobseeker can openly describe their skills, experiences and target job roles online but whilst you are still employed, any recruiter would expect you to display full loyalty to your organisation.

By the time they reach shortlisting, many recruiters look on the key professional networking sites to see how you present yourself online in a relevant public arena. For some more senior or specialist roles, they use the professional networking sites to draw up potential shortlists. Ask around your network about which professional networking sites are to be recommended for your target industries and have a look online and see how many people you can find who you already know. Instructions for setting up and developing your profile are on the home pages, but before you plunge in, get a feel for what a site offers and read carefully the profiles of everyone you know to identify what you think is a good presentation. The presentation templates are explicitly designed to be updated quickly, so as your confidence grows in using these sites, you can quickly add experiences or connections. Building up a profile on these sites is also good practice for developing your own CVs and as you update them, make sure that you keep them synchronised with your developing online profile. Remember that the golden rules of face-to-face networking also apply to developing your online network: always offer help and say thank you if someone can refer you on to one of their own contacts.

CONTACT NUMBERS

If you are currently employed, never use your work email address or phone number as a potential contact point for job searching. Do you really want your colleagues to overhear your half of a conversation confirming an interview appointment or spotting you sending off an email application to a recruiter? You also need to consider the moral implications of using your current workplace's internet provision for your personal career development.

Recruiters understand that voice-mail and email messages may have to wait until lunch break or early evening to be picked up. At minimum, however, they will expect you to be checking your personal emails and voice messages at least once a day: recruitment is a very fast-paced industry and you will be expected to be swiftly available on whatever contact routes you have given to the recruiter.

A small but significant part of your online self-presentation is a sensible email address. It is possible to launch yourself online with a free email address within minutes. Today's labour markets mean that you must be contactable online by recruiters; it is as important as having a phone number. When you set up an address, please don't create something silly, apparently witty to close friends or family or completely incomprehensible. If your current personal email address is a flippant reference, set up a different one now that you can use solely for jobseeking. Consider which address leaves the most professional impression on a potential recruiter:

jennyminesabottleofwine@emailprovider.co.uk or
jennysmith5983@emailprovider.co.uk.

I have seen such email addresses on several CVs.

Another point about phone calls is to ensure that you remain in control of what is discussed and when it is discussed. Once you have given out a personal number to recruiters, expect them to ring at any time. This might be as you are passing through a supermarket checkout, for example, or driving. Increasingly

when vacancies attract a large response, one way to pull out the stronger applicants is to ask questions over the phone. If you apply for any sort of customer service role, especially if phone work is a significant part of the role, then expect this to be an early part of the interview process. Never allow the recruiter to bounce you into a phone-based interview while you are distracted or in a public place. I have overheard half of some truly terrifying phone conversations while travelling on trains. You cannot give of your best to a phone interview if you are being distracted, overheard, or unable to reach your prepared notes on this application. If you are not ready to be interviewed, then make your apologies and say that it is extremely inconvenient. Most recruiters will regard a refusal to be put at a disadvantage as a point in your favour. Explain your current circumstances, politely request an arrangement to ring them back at a different time, ideally very soon, when you are in control of your notes, your phone and your time. The worst they can do is refuse to let you, and you have already bought yourself some thinking time and may now be within reach of a lay-by for a proper pause.

■ Checking how your job search fits into your long-term goals

Research does not just happen online or at network meetings; bright ideas can strike you when reflecting on your own in any circumstances. Many jobseekers I have worked with have found the following exercises helpful in terms of working out how they match what employers might be looking for and consequently, where profitable investigation could happen. These next activities are probably most helpful for those who are still hazy about what sort of role or industry is right for them but all jobseekers will benefit from considering the wider future for their long-term career goals. This is about thinking big and placing your job search into the national and local context.

The PEST TEST: Political, Economic, Social and Technological

This analysis tool has been around a long time and remains particularly useful for jobseekers at an early stage of job search or for testing the long-term viability of a particular business idea. I've worked on this process with jobseekers when it has enabled them to unearth significant decisions about changing the direction of their careers or changing industries in response to what they now see as changing local demand. I've seen it prompt decisions to emigrate, retrain and launch new businesses and a key part of its success, I think, is its simplicity: any jobseeker in any situation can find these questions helpful for testing and clarifying their long-term career goals.

Consider the following headings and in Exercise 3, on page 62, write down everything happening now under that category that may influence the world of paid employment and specifically your target industries over the next ten years. If the questions stump you, you will probably know someone in your networks who may be able to help you tackle these reflections. This is not a crystal ball or a tough exam in current affairs; it simply invites you to reflect on what is happening in the wider world and how current trends could affect the industries you are interested in exploring for future work.

Political covers international, national and local politics. What are the key policies being applied by the current ruling political party? How close are we to a general election? How likely is it that the current party would stay in power? If you think it is unlikely, then what are the opposition parties claiming they would change? What influence do local politicians of all parties have on local labour markets? How do all of these issues affect the world of work?

Economic covers the impact of both global businesses and small, local ones. What is happening to your local economy? Do you want to work in a specialist or niche market? Who buys the end products or services that you want to help produce and how likely is it that this market will expand, stagnate or contract over the next five years? How does your target industry interact with the national economy? Do you want to work in a business-to-business market or a business-to-consumer market and what does that imply for your customers?

Social covers trends that affect the whole of the population and could have national or international implications. For example, we know that across Europe we have a rapidly ageing population, which has huge implications for the future of the labour market: some industries catering for older generations will expand and we will all have to start adapting to new expectations of what retirement age means. How people live, with whom, in what sort of housing and how they spend their time and money will affect how we all work in a wide range of industries, from tourism to healthcare. What social trends do you see emerging for different generations in terms of lifestyle choices and restrictions?

Technological covers the impact of technology on our lives. It is perhaps the hardest of the PEST trends to predict; all we can say for certain is that the rate of change in the technology most of us use now on a daily basis will continue to accelerate. The technology industry has consistently made products obsolete at the rate of approximately every 9 to 18 months. The rise in the available applications of mobile devices has transformed expectations in many job roles, as well as our consumer demands from a wide range of products and services. How does your target industry apply technology now and how might this change over the next few years? What are the implications of constantly evolving technologies for your job search?

CASE STUDY

Predicting retail customer demand

Around 2000, I helped Joe develop his career plans by using many of the Chapter 1 activities and the PEST tool. As he built his PEST analysis, Joe grew more confident about his long-term plan: to combine his retail experience and his interest in plants by seeking work as a garden centre manager, then use his managerial experience to open his own garden centre business. His research about potential customers then identified what every visitor to a garden centre has noticed; the core market for garden centres is retired people. If I was working with Joe today, I predict that the number of relatively wealthy retirees with both time and money to spend on gardening products will be smaller than during the last decade. We have all heard about the need to work longer and the fragility of modern pensions.

I'd probably now suggest that the most likely expanding market in gardening retail would be 'grow your own' products. That might lead a modern Joe to research different routes to a fruit and veg based leisure business. Perhaps online retail might enable him to combine his past experience, personal interests and longer-term business ambitions.

Have a go at completing overleaf your reflections on these wide-ranging Political, Economic, Social and Technological questions in relation to your job search and identify which areas would be helpful to research further. If you want more space, then roll out some more wallpaper!

EXERCISE 3: Political, Social, Economic and Technological forecasting

POLITICAL

SOCIAL

ECONOMIC

TECHNOLOGICAL

■ SWOT Analysis

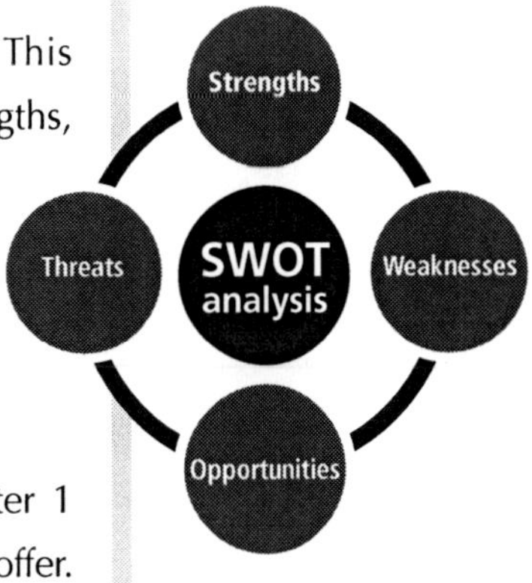

SWOT stands for Strengths, Weaknesses, Opportunities and Threats. This reflection tool asks you to consider what you think are your personal strengths, weaknesses (or development areas), opportunities and threats in relation to your job search. It is very helpful to complete this reflection before you start writing up your CV, as considering your strengths is a good springboard for presenting your key skills and achievements.

Start Exercise 4, page 65, by looking at all your work from the Chapter 1 exercises that helped you define the skills and experiences you have to offer. You have a unique set of strengths that no one else in the job market can precisely offer to a potential employer. The purpose of spending time on this self-analysis tool is to clarify just what your unique strengths are. Again, for each strength you put into Section A, try to think of evidence that you could use in a future interview to describe how you apply that strength.

Although this tool traditionally uses the word 'weaknesses', I don't use it when working with jobseekers on any activity. Positive language is vital when coaching anyone through a challenging task like finding and nailing the right job for them. The purpose of the second section (B) here is for you to assess what might be the biggest hindrances for you as you explore your target market. For example, if you think you want to change career and do something completely new, your key hindrance will be lack of demonstrable experience in your target job role. Similarly, if you want to work in an area that you haven't worked in for some time, then your key hindrance will be apparent lack of relevant, up-to-date experience. Under your hindrances, start to consider how you might limit their impact in your CV or interview presentation. There is more help on presenting your vulnerable areas favourably in Chapter 4 on page 118: for now, you are simply identifying what those areas might be in relation to a particular target industry or role and starting to note how you could balance them with more positive examples.

The third and fourth sections (C and D) ask you to consider the issues outside you that will affect your job search, along similar lines to a PEST analysis. In these sections, reflect on what is currently happening in your target industries or job roles that relates directly to your talents.

In the Opportunities section, the sky really is your limit. Again, start with your Chapter 1 work, which has now given you a clear sense of who you are, what you have to offer and what you are looking for. What sort of work, job role, employer and industry could be looking for your skills in the areas you want to work in? After considering your PEST results, what is happening in your locality or job market that may offer you an opportunity? What work do you really want to enjoy doing and which organisations are doing it? If starting your own business is important to you, then what is the gap in the market that you have identified?

In the Threats section, list the issues that could hamper your job search. The obvious issue to consider here is the competition; most vacancies currently attract a lot of applicants. It could be that you are trying to enter a profession that is still generating a high number of qualified graduates or that your local economy has just lost a large employer, increasing your local competition. Other threats could be that your target jobs are in a different part of the country to you or that a lot of businesses already offer customers a very similar service to the one you are planning.

Opposite on page 65 is a grid for completing your own SWOT analysis for your current target job search. It will give you more food for thought about where to start looking for potential work.

CASE STUDY

Spotting an opportunity

Sarah was made redundant from a bank and due to her family circumstances, she had to find work literally within walking distance of where she lived. She had worked in hotels earlier in her career and enjoyed customer service. While still employed at the bank, she completed several of the activities in this book, including a SWOT analysis. She had noticed on her walk to work a building project that was an expanding GP surgery; two practices were moving into renovated premises.

Sarah noted in her hindrances box that she had no health experience apart from being a patient but her strengths included a lot of customer service skills. She tailored her CV accordingly to boost her transferable experience (more on presenting transferable skills effectively in Chapter 3 on page 80). She practised her 'Meeting Prince Charles Speech', approached two of the GPs directly as she spotted them in the nearly finished building and politely expressed her interest in potential receptionist roles. She was granted an interview and subsequently offered a job, largely because the partners were impressed by her initiative and relevant customer service experience.

EXERCISE 4: SWOT Analysis

(A) STRENGTHS

Evidence

(B) HINDRANCES

How to balance them

(C) OPPORTUNITIES

(D) THREATS

To summarise what you have learned in this chapter about looking effectively, you now know that:

- ***Some, but crucially not all, vacancies are advertised on organisations' websites or in trade, local or national press, or with recruitment agencies.***
- ***Uncovering 'hidden jobs' requires diligent research and focused networking.***
- ***Networking is a natural skill that can be developed with practice by every jobseeker.***
- ***Employers do look favourably on jobseekers who have made tailored direct approaches, as these applicants demonstrate the ability to take the initiative.***
- ***Effective customised applications show a potential employer that you can research, analyse, present information well and sell yourself.***
- ***If you sell yourself well, then you are likely to sell your future employer well, which makes you a candidate worthy of further investigation.***

Recruiters do take note of the application that stands out from the crowd: in the next chapter, you will learn how to do exactly that for your application.

CHAPTER 3

Making an impressive application

... that earns you an interview

By the end of this chapter, you will be able to:

- ***Build an effective portfolio of CVs and use them appropriately.***
- ***Apply in a style that will make the right impression on a recruiter.***
- ***Seize control of an organisational application form.***
- ***Read between the lines of job descriptions and person specifications to ensure that you demonstrate how well you match the vacancy.***
- ***Write an attractive covering letter to support direct applications and in response to advertised vacancies.***
- ***Manage recruitment agencies to work effectively for you.***
- ***Prepare for potential self-employment by impressing the bank manager.***
- ***Get onto the interview shortlist.***

By this point in your job hunt, you have a clear idea of what you have to offer your next employer, what you want out of your next job and who might be the right employer to have that opportunity for you. You now need to prepare your sales brochure, or CV, to put in front of the decision makers.

CVs are also called 'resumes' in some countries *(see CV box, below)*. Despite their different names and appearances, their purposes remain the same. They present your skills and experiences to an employer in a manner that demonstrates how well you fit the vacancy you are targeting. If you keep this core purpose in mind when writing your CV, then your content and layout will always suit your application. There are some golden rules to building an effective CV that remain the same, regardless of the precise appearance of your unique CVs.

WHAT IS A CV?

Your CV is simply the document that makes a recruiter decide to either reject you or invite you for a discussion about this vacancy. CV stands for curriculum vitae, which is Latin for 'the race or course of my life'. You may also come across the word 'resume' from the French, meaning a summary, pronounced 'resumay'. Resume is often used by organisations of European or North American origin.

■ CVs: The golden rules

Perhaps the first principle to stress is your need for CVs, plural. I always work with jobseekers to help them build a core CV, which they then adjust by varying amounts for each application that they make. It is vital that you begin the process of writing your CV with this aim of creating a core CV which then generates customised CVs. Too many CVs cross recruiters' screens or desks that are flat and vague because their owner assumes that they only have one profile to present to every potential employer. This panicky approach results in inappropriate prominence of particular skills or experiences and consequently their interview strike rate is low. It is very quickly clear to the experienced recruiter when a jobseeker has only prepared one CV for all applications. It is also a terrible waste of time and energy to scatter your work across many applications. The holistic approach of our coaching at *Nail That Job* is to enable jobseekers to focus their search on the right job for them, which inevitably means being selective in your jobseeking and selective in your self-presentation. Your time and energy is better spent on polishing each separate application from your core or master CV to fit the key demands of that job.

Honesty

Don't lie; your sins will find you out. If you are untruthful on your CV or application form about any aspect of your past experience and you are subsequently offered the job, you will have a shock when you read the small print on your job contract. (Every job offer will be accompanied by a contract, which is a legal requirement for every employer.) This is because standard job contracts have a sentence that reads something like this:

> *"By signing to accept this job offer, I confirm that to the best of my knowledge, all the information I have supplied is correct and that if it is subsequently discovered to be inaccurate, I could be dismissed for gross misconduct."*

The implication of this statement is that if you start work and then some aspect of your references, qualifications or past roles as claimed by you on your CV prove to be untrue, you can be sacked immediately. I encourage jobseekers to ensure that they present all their relevant skills, attributes and experiences to the prospective employer as favourably as possible, WHILE REMAINING TRUTHFUL AT ALL TIMES. Issues such as gaps in employment or delicate reasons for leaving previous jobs can always be presented honestly and positively, even if they were unpleasant experiences for you at the time. If you were last looking for employment some time ago, you may be cheered to know that recruiters view gaps in paid employment or frequent job changes more favourably than perhaps in earlier years. They will want to understand the context of your past career choices (or accidental choices) when they ask you for interview and will probably want to explore these with you in more detail. Have a look at page 121 in Chapter 4 about preparing answers to difficult questions.

CHASING UP REFERENCES

Recruiters also tend to chase up references and check the information that you provide more thoroughly than in the past, so start writing your CVs in the knowledge that your information will be checked by someone at some later stage in the recruitment process.

Appearance

The layout of any CV must be smooth and uncluttered with plenty of white space around your typing. When planning the layout, keep an eye on the overall impact of the final document, and consider what it looks like on screen as well as paper. Choose a clean, simple font that is easy on the eye; a good test is to ask a mature person who needs reading glasses to glance at it and see if they think the finished document looks crowded or lopsided. I don't recommend any particular font but all of us recruiters have our preferences; your mission is to keep it clear. Please keep to one, or at the most two, fonts to sub-divide information and ensure consistency of appearance across headings and subheadings. Using one font for everything and applying bold to create highlights, usually achieves a smoother effect than mixing fonts. I'd recommend not using any font size smaller than 12 point no matter how many words you think you need to squash into the document.

The size of your CV

You may have heard about strict rules on the number of pages expected. Some recruiters will explicitly demand no more than two sides and some simply expect no more than two sides. As with any instruction given to you in an application process, **please follow it to the letter** and ensure that your CV is no more than two sides if required. This can be restrictive for some older people, or anyone who has a wide range of experiences to offer. If you are in these categories and are not explicitly restricted to two sides, then look for a balance between a target of two sides (including plenty of white space) and ensuring that you include the correct content to support your application. Using bullet points rather than full paragraphs can make good use of limited space. I do start to lose heart when I see that I have to read more than three sides of information about an individual to make that decision about whether it is worth the time to meet them in person.

Don't waste white space by starting with the heading:

My Name, Curriculum Vitae

Everyone reading this document knows what it is and the space demanded by the words Curriculum Vitae will work harder for you as white space. It is also rare to see that title spelled correctly. As a passing comment on white space, please keep your paper CVs to white or cream paper; I have tried to read paper CVs on pink, yellow, pale green and pale blue paper. Please just visualise a tired recruiter whose reading glasses may need adjustment, working in dim light trying to make a decision about interviewing you. Make sure that the physical appearance of your CV paints you, literally, in the best possible light.

Need for proofreading

Proofread everything at least three times more than you think you need before you press the send button or lick the envelope. A fresh pair of trusted eyes is always welcome if you can show your completed application to someone before you send it off. It is astonishing how many times you can read over a document and your brain misses your typing error that jumps out at anyone who didn't type the original. I always recommend completing any application well before the advertised cut-off date, putting it away for at least one day and night, then taking it out again to re-read freshly. Jobseekers tell me how helpful they find this simple discipline and how frequently the rested eyes see potential for improvement before sending off the completed application well within the deadline. If you are not a confident speller, then spellcheck will do most of the work for you. What it can't do is identify misspelled words with different meanings that sound the same, i.e. 'their' and 'there' or 'whether' and 'weather'. Your computer will also check the punctuation for you, usually accurately and it can make less reliable suggestions to change your grammar. I do ask that you check that your computer is working in UK English, not US English. I cannot emphasise too much how many times recruiters see spelling mistakes on a daily basis. Even if written communication is not a vital requirement for the job, the fact that an applicant can't be bothered to check suggests that they don't care enough about my vacancy to deserve an interview.

Presenting referees

Ask your referees before you send out your first application if they would be prepared to support your application and have their contact details circulated amongst your target employers. Opinions differ on how appropriate it is to include your referees' contact details on your CV. I would usually suggest keeping all referees off your CV unless you are young and struggling to use the space wisely. If the name of one referee will help your second page look balanced, then leave it in. Recruiters expect that by the time they make conditional offers, then every selected candidate will have the contact details of two referees to put forward immediately.

Please keep your referees updated on your jobseeking progress so that they are not surprised by an email or phone call asking for the reference. In order to keep the recruiting process on track, referees are usually initially contacted by phone or email to offer an informal assessment of your work. If the recruiter likes what they hear, then a formal written request for a reference will follow. Most job offers come with a clause specifying that:

> *"This job offer is subject to the receipt of satisfactory references . . ."*

which means that you have not yet completed the selection process. Rarely, I have chosen to withdraw conditional job offers on the basis of information I received from referees and this is typical of most recruiters' experience.

The function of a referee is to provide the recruiter with additional information about the preferred candidate that should confirm details already supplied by that candidate. They must not be related to you but know you well enough to be able to make an informed comment about your character, work performance or attitude to work. It would be expected that at least one referee would be your current employer, but recruiters understand that sometimes there may be appropriate reasons for not listing your current employer as a referee. Recruiters do not contact current employers until we have the permission of the candidate to do so, so that we do not reveal to an employer that one of their staff is looking for another job: you have to remain in control of the timing of that conversation. There are valid reasons for choosing not to nominate your current employer as a referee and if you have been selected as the preferred candidate, recruiters are always happy to talk through with you the reasons why. Any candidate in that position would be expected to provide a valid alternative referee who could make accurate comments about their recent work performance.

WHAT IS A TESTIMONIAL?

A testimonial is not the same as a reference and should not be stapled to your CV as additional material. A testimonial is written by someone who has worked with you in the past as an open letter to anyone who may read it in the future. It vouches for having seen you display certain core positive behaviours. It is not written at the request of a recruiter needing specific evidence of your past performance and consequently is not highly valued by recruiters. If asked for two references, then one reference and a testimonial is not usually acceptable.

There has been a debate in the recruitment industry about the true value of a reference from existing or past employers. Some knotty legal cases about the impact of negative but accurate – or even positive but inaccurate – references have provoked interesting results for both jobseekers and employers. Consequently some employers are now pretty wary of providing anything more detailed than confirmation of the job roles held by the candidate, the dates of employment and possibly records of sick days taken.

Recruiters also face problems in chasing references from foreign, bankrupt or failed organisations where the old employer no longer exists. If you have to provide references for past work with a now defunct organisation, then try to find any person who did work with you and could make a relevant comment on your work. Please clarify for the recruiter what your relationship with this referee was at the extinct organisation. Whoever you ask to act as your referee, please set them up to be ready to support you before you start building your CVs.

■ Content of CVs

Here comes the exciting bit: planning your core sales brochure using those golden rules. This is where you seize control of the recruitment process by selecting the right information about yourself that best matches your target vacancy. The expected formats for CVs are either:

- **the reverse chronological layout**, which presents your most recent experience at the top of the page and then works backwards in time towards your earliest qualifications ***or***
- **the functional layout**, which groups your experience in terms of skills or competences that are key requirements for your target role in order of their relevance, rather than in the order in which you learned them.

Take a quick look ahead to page 76 to scan the CV of a fictional jobseeker, Wendy Smith and see how the two different formats look for her. The route you choose depends on your preferences and experiences. Most jobseekers are more familiar with the reverse chronological layout but you may be better served by presenting your skills in the functional layout. It is particularly helpful if you are older, with a wide range of experiences or if you want to showcase skills that you haven't applied for some time. One is not better than the other: the reverse chronological is more common than the functional but choose the one that suits your job search best. Some recent research from the University of London suggests that recruiters look first at your most recent employment history, then read on to your personal summary statement but this could be because we see more examples of the reverse chronological CV in any one recruiting day.

TIP

You might spend time wisely by writing up your experience using both formats and then compare the results. You could also see if a different layout changes the overall impact of your CV.

Whichever format you use, the **top third of the page** must grab my attention quickly and already prompt me to visualise how well you match your target role. Start with your **name and contact details**, remember the points made in Chapter 2, page 58 about choosing the right phone and email contacts. The jury is still out on whether to include a small '**head and shoulders**' photograph of yourself as part of your initial contact information. I am seeing more and more CVs recently with photos included, probably as it has become so much easier to import a small photo into documents. Personally, I don't want a photo, as I want to focus on a candidate's description of what they have to offer in order to decide whether I invite them to interview. I am also nervous about whether a photo might subconsciously distract me from making a truly

objective decision. Some large-scale recruitment exercises could ask you to include your photo to help manage a long process. When large numbers are involved, a snapshot of a candidate's face helps to track them through the recruitment. Some older or black and ethnic minority applicants are nervous about the possibility of recruiter distraction from fair assessment that a photo might provoke. If you do decide to add a snapshot, then please borrow the best amateur photographer that you know and ask them to use their best quality equipment. Make sure you are relaxed and wearing business clothes with brushed hair in front of a calm background. Check that they take pictures at the right resolution: online photos demand a different resolution from paper photos, so you always have the risk that an electronic application might be printed off at some point onto paper and blur your carefully posed photo.

Immediately below your **name and contact details**, I need to read a **brief summary** of what you have to offer and how this makes you unique. I'd prefer to read this as a couple of sentences rather than bullet points, as the sentences will also tell me how skilled you are at written work. The language here should be positive and action oriented, focusing on what you have achieved at work. Above all, it must read as *you*, not a collection of words you found on someone else's CV and thought they sounded good. Recruiters can always sniff out insincerity. This is the hardest bit of a CV to get right and taking your time, reviewing and asking for feedback from trusted friends, will pay dividends here. The purpose of these couple of sentences is to set out clearly who you are and what you could offer the target job. You might find it easier to prepare once you have completed the rest of the CV. It won't change very much from one application to the next, as this in effect describes the essence of you. Your 'Meeting Prince Charles Speech' *(see Chapter 1, page 31)* will be a helpful springboard here to clarifying what you have to offer.

After your summary, you will be listing either:

- **your most recent skills and achievements** if you have opted for the reverse chronological, ***or***
- **your most relevant** if you are going down the functional route.

Group them in paragraphs representing one job or one cluster of related skills/experiences. It is hard to give typical space estimates here, but older people with more experiences to note are probably well into the second page by the time all relevant achievements have been logged. The adjective 'relevant' is key here, regardless of your age. If in doubt about the level of detail you want to cover, leave it to headlines and be ready to describe your examples in more detail at interview. The white space left will always work to your advantage. There is a vital exercise for you on page 82 to help you clarify what an achievement is and how to describe it productively on your CV. If you go for the purely functional route, then you do need to list a summary of your employment in bullet points: just one line per job role in reverse chronological order, job title and name of employer.

If you are not currently in paid employment, then it is of huge advantage to have a voluntary post to describe at the top of your list. Recruiters will immediately be focused on the fact that you are at least keeping the habits of work going while contributing to a good cause. The best sort of voluntary work to be engaged in is something that develops your skills, links in some way to your target role and keeps up your morale.

Consider how you present any piece of information on your CV in terms of jargon. What is obvious technical knowledge for you might be jargon to the recruiter. This is particularly important to check if you are seeking fresh industries and are trying to describe skills, achievements or qualifications that won't mean much to anyone working outside that industry. If in doubt, then spell out any industry acronyms, e.g. Point of Sale instead of POS, rather than risk littering your CV with what might be seen as random groups of initials.

After your key experiences, skills and achievements, it is helpful to list your qualifications: always the most recent first and any other relevant experiences such as travelling, volunteering or personal interests. The final couple of lines should be the name, phone or email contact details of your key referee and an explanation of how they know you and your work. Your measure for what to include and what to leave out should always be the test of how well it shows your match to your target job.

The best way to visualise how all this information works together is to offer you an example CV. What follows is fictional and please see it a guide and inspiration, not a template to copy slavishly: my key message is to make the pattern your own. Over the page is our fictional jobseeker, Wendy and a suggestion for presenting her CV in both reverse chronological and functional layouts.

EXAMPLE: REVERSE CHRONOLOGICAL CV

WENDY SMITH

07773 567890 (personal mobile)

Wendy@anyemail.co.uk
27, Acacia Avenue
Felpersham
Borsetshire BO27 8NO

A self-motivated organiser and administrator with strong experience of customer-facing roles and proven ability to remain calm under pressure and achieve tight deadlines. Actively seeking a full-time opportunity to utilise first-class numeracy and customer communication skills.

CAREER HISTORY

Sales support administrator (part time) with Bricks & Mortar Estate Agents
From (date) to (date)

- Prompt and accurate production of property sales leaflets using Estates Design Elastic Rooms software program
- Face-to-face and phone customer liaison
- Successfully reconciled all account queries each month by monitoring payments
- Re-organised office filing system to reduce time taken to collate clients' viewing records
- Achieved all personal targets set by manager at annual appraisal

Career break to bring up family
From (date) to (date)

Clinic Receptionist at Borsetshire Hospital, Manor Road, Felpersham
From (date) to (date)

- Welcomed patients and registered them onto the Where's My Patient Gone? program, sending them to the correct clinic waiting area
- Liaised with local GPs, their staff and professional hospital colleagues to ensure proper maintenance of confidential records
- Booked patients into the appropriate clinics as requested by medical staff and managed changes to appointments where necessary

Accounts Clerk at Felpersham Engineering Ltd, 19 Forge Street, Felpersham

From (date) to (date)

- Sole support for Accounts Manager with full responsibility for 61 supplier accounts using the Give Me The Loot software program
- Successfully reduced account discrepancies by 4% by improving the account tracking process
- Maintained up to date supplier records, liaising with partner accounts colleagues across Europe
- Provided accurate and timely weekly, monthly and quarterly reports to senior managers

EARLY EXPERIENCE

Initial accounts administration and receptionist experience gained through Temps 'R' Us agency, High Street, Felpersham

QUALIFICATIONS

RSA; CLAIT	*(Computer Literacy and Information Technology)*	Date
GNVQ	Business Administration	Date
A level	Statistics C	Date
	Geography C	Date
	Maths D	Date

TRAINING

Specialist Programs as outlined above
Microsoft Excel, Word, Outlook,
First Aid Certificate, current until (date)
Health and Safety

INTERESTS

Volunteer for the Ambridge Wildlife Trust, counting a range of migratory species, cross stitch and badminton player for Borsetshire Ladies League

PERSONAL REFEREE

Linda Snell, past HR Manager, Borsetshire Hospital
linda@ambridgevillage.co.uk

EXAMPLE: FUNCTIONAL CV

WENDY SMITH

07773 567890 *(personal mobile)*
Wendy@anyemail.co.uk
27, Acacia Avenue
Felpersham
Borsetshire BO27 8NO

A self-motivated organiser and administrator with strong experience of customer-facing roles and proven ability to remain calm under pressure and achieve tight deadlines. Actively seeking a full-time opportunity to utilise first-class numeracy and customer communication skills.

EXPERIENCE AND ACHIEVEMENTS

Personal attributes:

- Proven ability to communicate with a wide range of people sensitively and with discretion through face to face, phone and electronic media
- Confident teamworking with a range of professional colleagues in healthcare and commercial industry
- Productive sales and negotiating skills applied to client and supplier relationships, regularly exceeding sales targets by average of 3%
- Willing to work the hours necessary to complete the task in hand, with a record of exceeding annual performance targets

Accounting:

- Reduced outstanding debts by 10% by improving accounting procedures for monitoring clients
- Reduced supplier tracking costs by 4% through simplifying supplier record keeping system
- Effectively analysed financial data to minimise costs and maximise sales opportunities

Computing:

- Successfully developed in-house systems to improve time and cost benefits
- Confident application of Excel spread sheets to produce statistical reports for senior managers
- Typing speeds up to 60wpm to produce high quality sales and branding materials under tight deadlines

SUMMARY OF EMPLOYMENT

Current role Sales support administrator Bricks & Mortar Estate Agents, since (date)

Borsetshire Hospital Clinic Receptionist, from (date) to (date)

Felpersham Engineering Ltd Accounts Clerk, from (date) to (date)

Temps 'R' Us, Felpersham Temporary accounting and administration roles, from (date) to (date)

QUALIFICATIONS

RSA, CLAIT	*(Computer Literacy and Information Technology)*		Date
GNVQ	Business Administration		Date
A level	Statistics	C	Date
	Geography	C	Date
	Maths	D	Date

TRAINING

Specialist Programs as outlined above
Microsoft Excel, Word, Outlook,
First Aid Certificate, current until (date)
Health and Safety

INTERESTS

Volunteer for the Ambridge Wildlife Trust, counting a range of migratory species, cross stitch and badminton player for Borsetshire Ladies League

PERSONAL REFEREE

Linda Snell, past HR Manager, Borsetshire Hospital
linda@ambridgevillage.co.uk

■ Building your own CV

Now that you have looked at examples for both a reverse chronological and a functional CV, it is time to start building your own. Have another look at your work in Chapter 1 on the competences you have demonstrated throughout your career and keep that in front of you for this next exercise. The kernel of any CV is demonstrating what you have done for past employers/volunteer activities/study and being able to indicate the impact that your work has had. When I'm recruiting, I am impressed by candidates who know their achievements, can describe them objectively and even quantify the impact of their work. That suggests to me that they are the candidates who could make an impact on my organisation too. You will have noticed that Wendy was able to put numbers to her achievements to demonstrate how much more efficient her ideas had made the organisation. By the time I have skimmed the first page, I have a clear message that Wendy has delivered improvements for her past employers. So, how do you identify the key achievements in your work and learning that have given demonstrable benefits to the organisations you worked for?

A structure that many jobseekers I work with have found very useful is the **CAR** framework:

Challenge or Issue: what was the situation?
Action: what did you do to improve the situation?
Results: what difference did your actions make?

Frequently, people find this section of a CV difficult to start because they either see it as showing off, or too small an achievement to be worthy of note, simply what they are expected to do for basic pay. It is also common to start practising this exercise using a lot of 'we' instead of 'I'. You must eliminate the word 'we' from your job search language and start clarifying the individual contribution that you made to any project. Even if there are another 999 people in your large organisation with the same job title as you, you all make 1000 unique contributions to that organisation as you carry out your daily tasks. By the time you reach interview, you must be able to describe confidently the impact that you have had on past work, not hide behind 'we' or 'the team' or 'our' or 'us' or 'they'; *see Chapter 4, page 126.*

Start by considering all the possible opportunities that you have to show off to a future employer from your past studies, volunteer activities, structured leisure activities, travelling experiences, managing family and household or paid employment. The less paid employment experience you have to offer, the more widely you need to spread your net for examples to start polishing. How and in what situations did you make a difference? Go back to your first exercise in this book in Chapter 1 on page 9 where you identified evidence of when you displayed various competences. You may be able to think of some more examples by now. Take your five strongest examples and write them into the CAR grid overleaf. There are more blank boxes after the first five for you to add more key competences if you are now targeting a specific application. You can always return to the wallpaper, *(see page 20)* if you need more room. This is where you start using your research on your target vacancy from Chapter 2 to identify the key competences that the recruiter is looking for in this vacancy. You might also find some strong examples to develop here from your first WOW map of skills, competences and tasks that you are good at that you completed on page 21 in Chapter 1. The more recent the achievement the better, but make your final selection of examples based on relevance to the core competences rather than recent ones.

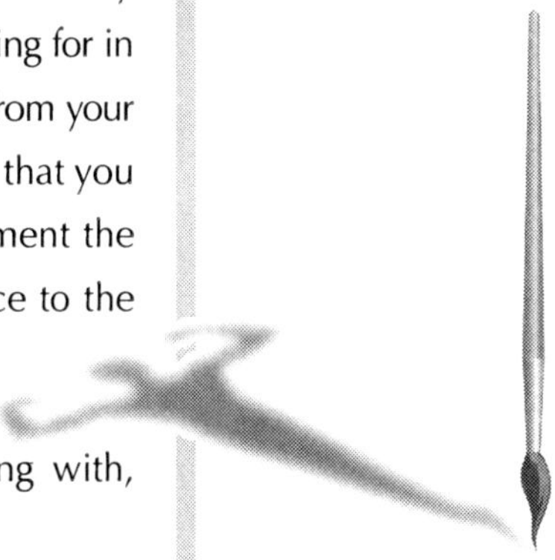

Remember that **Challenge** describes the situation you were dealing with, probably one that was out of the ordinary for a regular day of work.
Paint the picture of the task you had to deal with.

In the **Action** box, describe precisely what you did to make a difference. Do not use 'we' or 'they'. The whole purpose of this exercise is to clarify *your* achievements at work.

In the **Results** box, list the benefits that your actions achieved for the organisation. If you have some numbers of any kind to put in here, that will look good on your CV. Results could be time and/or money saved; additional sales made; better quality products or customer service; positive comments from customers; quicker or better processes; lower costs, wastage, accident or error rates; design improvements; any kind of external recognition or award; new skills learned; and new products, services or ideas generated, etc.

The final section of this grid, the **Summary Sentence,** is your space to polish up that story you have just put together into one, action-oriented, articulate sentence. This is what arrives on your CV under your key skills and achievements section. It could also be the springboard for your personal summary. Make sure that you choose words that still sound right for you. You can find free thesauruses online, or the old-fashioned sort in a library.

TIP

For anyone who struggles to choose the right word when writing, a thesaurus is a vital tool. If you've never used one before, it is not a newly discovered dinosaur but a magnificent list of words grouped by similar meanings. For example, if you want to write something like 'I did this...', look up 'do' in the index and you will be pointed at many more interesting verbs, which will bring your achievement summary alive.

EXERCISE 1: Identifying and summarising your achievements				
EVIDENCE OF MY WORK	COMPETENCE 1	COMPETENCE 2	COMPETENCE 3	COMPETENCE 4
CHALLENGE				
ACTION				
RESULT				
SUMMARY SENTENCE				

COMPETENCE 5	COMPETENCE 6	COMPETENCE 7	COMPETENCE 8	COMPETENCE 9

■ Getting the most out of an application form

Some recruitment processes ask you to complete an organisational application form rather than a CV. You might think it worth sending back the application form with a CV if you don't think that the form enabled you to do yourself full justice and you were not specifically prohibited from sending one in. Commonly, large organisations have a standard form that is sent out for every job, regardless of the scope of that job, which can make it difficult to cover everything you want to under their headings. The key disadvantage of any application form is that you have now lost control of your self-presentation: you have to describe yourself under their headings in the order they want the information.

Recently, use of application forms has increased as recruiters try to simplify the analysis of large numbers of candidates. When every candidate is mapped out to the same format, it is easier to pick out who most closely matches your job specifications and you can be more confident that you are truly choosing without discrimination. There has been a longer history of using application forms and not accepting CVs in the public and voluntary sector. Like CVs, some golden rules apply to get the most out of them and most of the golden rules for CVs, also apply to application forms.

Application forms – the Golden Rules

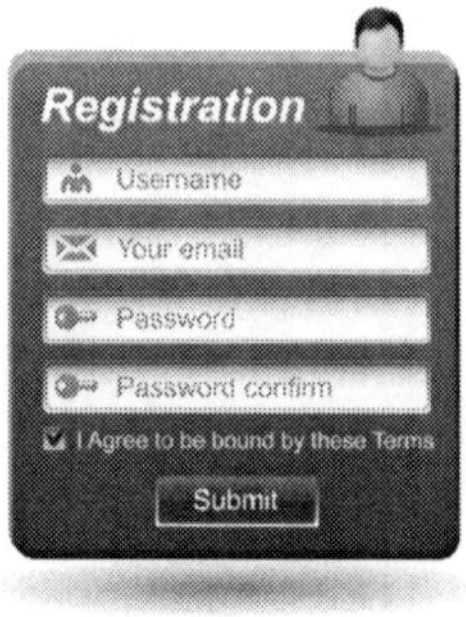

First of all, practise, so if you start with a paper copy, then copy another couple of versions of the empty form to practise how much space you will need. If it is an online form, then download a blank version, save it as a separate document in your system and practise on that first. I have heard of candidates practising online without saving a back up and then websites or computers crash and all information is lost, or the website send button gets pressed accidentally and incomplete forms are sent off.

Read the questions carefully. Follow every instruction to the letter. If you are asked to write in black ink, then blue might get your form thrown onto the 'No' heap without even reading the detail. I have done that myself when recruiting. If a candidate can't follow the simple instruction about colour of ink, then how effective are they likely to be in my vacancy? Black ink scans more clearly than blue in lower-powered scanners, so if the organisation requests it, then please help out everyone involved in the administration of the recruitment. Similarly, a request for block capitals is a plea for legible handwriting on paper versions of forms. Recruiters still regularly deal with hard-to-read writing, which will simply irritate the recruiter with a headache, regardless of how appropriate the illegible words are.

Read the questions carefully. If you are asked to send in **supporting information**, such as copies of driving licence, qualifications, proof of work permits, or separate diversity monitoring forms, then please check carefully and send in all requested extra information stapled to the main form. Check that you have completed accurately all the boring bits such as contact details for yourself and your referee(s) and signed and dated any paper form. Read the small print carefully at the signature section or, when online, you tick the box to say that you have read and agreed with the small print. This will be the legal bit to confirm that you have completed the form truthfully.

Read all the questions carefully and answer them all truthfully. Enough said.

Read the questions and your answers carefully. **Proofreading is vital** to correct any typos or punctuation errors that have crept in. Just as with a CV, try to find a willing and responsible volunteer to be your fresh pair of eyes before you send off the form. The white space around your words is just as important as for a CV, hence the need to practise. If completing a paper version, and you need more space in a box, then add a note directing the reader to the separate sheet of paper and continue on a fresh sheet that gets securely stapled onto the form. The recruiter would rather read another sheet than wrestle with tiny, scrawled writing that was a desperate attempt to squash everything in. Most online forms will have fields to complete that allow you to expand the box. In the unlikely event that you need more space in an online application, then neatly direct the reader to a different, relevant box that has spare space. Never leave any box blank in case the recruiter thinks you have forgotten it. If any question does not apply to you, simply write or type 'N/A', which stands for 'not applicable'.

Read all the questions carefully and assemble all your supporting information about this job that you have discovered; e.g. job descriptions, organisational information, etc. before you start completing the form. Use your core CV as the basis for the application and set yourself the target of ensuring that you mention all your core achievements somewhere in the form. The most significant questions on the form for you to focus on will be worded something like:

Give an example of a situation when you displayed the following competence

And

Describe why you want to work for this organisation

And

Describe what you could bring to this organisation

These are the questions where you wrest back control of the form from the recruiter and ensure that your unique contributions shine out. Typically, candidates complete these sorts of questions poorly. Having read to this point in *Nail That Job*, you know how to describe your key skills, attributes, experiences and motivations clearly and you will stand out from the bulk of applicants. Many people are daunted by the white spaces of an application form and tend to waffle. Stay focused on the competence evidence that you know the recruiter is looking for and how you can demonstrate that you have that experience. Your Challenge, Action, Results framework will help you to structure your thoughts here. Have a look at page 120 in Chapter 4 for more ideas about how to answer the question: 'Why do you want to work for us?'

Some forms you complete could be initially sifted online by looking for key words. Your research will have indicated which words are key for this vacancy's competences and these sorts of questions are where the computer should find them in your application. Keep practising and re-drafting as many times as you need to in order to get your answers strong, positive and clear in these sections.

You will have noticed a theme in these golden rules for application forms about reading the questions carefully. I've read too many application forms where candidates have simply not answered the question. Either they genuinely misunderstood what was being asked of them or they were unable to describe their experience clearly in terms of evidence of relevant competences. Fellow recruiters agree with me that a significant proportion of application forms read as muddled or vague. A core task in your proofreading is to be checking that you have actually provided the information that has been asked for. If you do have a complex career history and on completion of the form, think that it hasn't allowed you to fully shine as much as you wanted to, then you have a final opportunity to present your key skills in your covering letter or email, *see page 99*. Before you put the form into your envelope or press the send button, save a copy of what you send off for your own records, to help you prepare for the interview that will shortly follow.

■ Reading Job Descriptions and Person Specifications accurately

At several points in your job search, I have already referred you to the use of job descriptions and person specifications as vital sources of information about your target job. If you have little work experience so far, these documents may still be mysterious to you. A vital skill for the jobseeker is to read between the lines of these documents, because they are the heart of the design of the recruitment process that you are entering. As such, they tell you precisely what the recruiter is looking for, suggest to you how close you are to that role and indicate how you can best present your application for this role by adjusting your core CV.

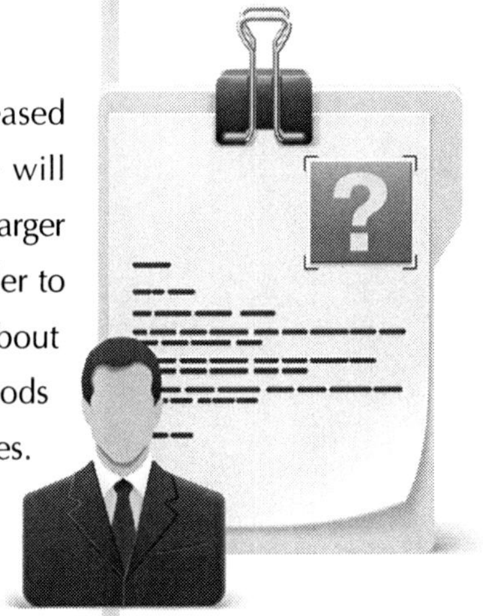

When any organisation decides that it has a vacancy, no money is released to recruit anyone until there is agreement about what the vacant role will achieve for the organisation. Normally this is an easy decision to make in larger organisations where recruitment is usually about adding a new jobholder to already existing jobs. Commonly in small organisations, (fewer than about 40 people) roles are more fluid and can vary a great deal over short periods of time, so job descriptions will probably have to be invented for new roles. Regardless of the size of the organisation or the job, a job description captures what the new jobholder will be paid to do. This clarity is vital to the recruiter, as the list of tasks the jobholder must achieve then determines what key skills, experiences or attributes will best fulfil that role.

The list of essential skills, attributes and experiences becomes the target person specification and describes the ideal jobholder that the recruiter is now looking for. Recruiters know that they are unlikely to find one individual with all those desired skills, experiences and attributes, but the person specification (usually shortened to person spec) becomes the template for the recruitment process and they will assess all candidates against these criteria. The successful jobseeker makes sure that their research uncovers this job description and person spec and then builds their application around the same template that the recruiter is using. Most advertised vacancies will supply the job description as a core part of the recruitment information made available to all candidates and it is very common in the public sector to be given a copy of the person specification as well. It is much harder to uncover the person spec when you are targeting speculative roles.

Over the next few pages, you can read some sample job descriptions and person specs for live jobs currently being carried out in three different organisations:

- a not-for-profit housing association
- a legal practice and
- a council

You can use these as examples to pick out the clues about the key things to emphasise in your CV or application form. You can see immediately that there is tremendous variation in the way organisations lay out this information and the degree of detail on offer to candidates. Only one example has a separate heading 'Person specification' and this example also tells you how each particular job requirement will be assessed through the application process. The content of these job descriptions hints at the sorts of behaviours required of these jobholders. As you read them, you can start to consider how it might feel to work there. There may be some language on these job descriptions that is jargon to you:

Safe guarding means that all the work undertaken should focus on the outcome of keeping vulnerable tenants safe

KPI stands for Key Performance Indicators, which are the success measures for a job role or a department

A fee earner is the technical name for the solicitors in a legal practice

Commensurate with means appropriate to that role

JOB PROFILE

SAMPLE 1
HOUSING ASSOCIATION

JOB TITLE: Support Service Advisor
JOB FAMILY: Support Family

Job purpose

- Proactively provides support to cluster team to enable the delivery of quality services that meet the contractual requirements

Key accountabilities

- Collate and use data to support team deliver contractual and business requirements
- A point of contact for customers (either by phone or in person)
- General administration and office support duties
- Attend visits as required (joint visits or to cover absence)
- Work in partnership with local agencies to ensure delivery of appropriate services to customers
- Support the team to ensure office environments are equipped appropriately and have a welcoming and customer focused environment
- Perform other reasonable additional duties at the request of the line manager

Skills and knowledge

Basic (1) Working (2) Detailed (3)

Health & Safety	2
Key working	1
Understanding the Association	2
Housing Management	1
Referral and assessment	2
Risk assessment	1
Individual support plans	1
Safe guarding	2
Money advice and budgeting	1
Customer involvement	2
Administration	3
Information Technology	2

Qualifications and experience

- Need to be able to demonstrate experience of organising, planning, administrative and meeting deadline skills

Key measures

- Contribution to achieving service outcomes, targets and service excellence KPIs
- Accuracy and timeliness of administration
- Audit outcomes
- Feedback from partner agencies (quality of relationship)
- Colleague feedback
- Line management assessment

How we do things

Colleague expectations

- Demonstrates a great positive attitude
- Shows consistent integrity, trust and fairness and embraces equality and diversity
- Delivers time after time
- Makes a difference every day
- Uses good judgement and initiative to find solutions
- Committed to learning and being the best through continual learning and development

JOB DESCRIPTION

SAMPLE 2
LEGAL PRACTICE

Job Title: Secretary
Department:
Location:
Reporting to:
Supervisory Responsibilities:

1 Job Summary

To provide secretarial and administrative assistance to one or more fee earners/managers within the firm

Neat and accurate audio and copy typing of letters, memos, forms and other documentation

Ensure that all documentation is named, saved and filed in accordance with the firm's guidelines.

Liaising with clients and other professionals in a courteous, discreet and businesslike manner

Taking accurate messages in a legible form and offering assistance whenever possible.

Answering ringing telephones within the department and taking brief messages, particular attention being paid to names and telephone numbers.

Ensuring that accurately completed work meets required deadlines

Assisting other fee earners and colleagues during periods of absence of members of the secretarial staff

Liaising with other members of the firm and offering assistance to ensure the efficiency and continuity of work flow

Making appointments and maintaining fee earner's diary

2 Job Requirements

Answering ringing telephones within the department and taking brief messages – particular attention being paid to names and telephone numbers

Ensuring that accurately completed work meets required deadlines

Assisting colleagues during periods of absence of members of the Admin team

Liaising with other members of the firm and offering assistance to ensure the efficiency and continuity of work flow

Working in accordance with procedures laid down in the Staff Handbook, meeting documented and implied quality standards within the firm

Ensuring safe keeping of client's files, deeds, wills etc. by maintaining filing system and up-to-date records

Presenting a well-groomed appearance and courteous manner at all times

Ensuring that the post room is kept clean and tidy and that the area presents a safe working environment

Ensuring that up-to-date instruction manuals/instruction sheets are readily accessible in case they are needed by staff who are not familiar with the equipment

Ensuring that machinery is treated with respect, e.g. photocopiers

Prompt time-keeping

Assisting with any other duties, using initiative when necessary, to ensure the smooth running of the office

Dealing with all matters in a confidential manner

Assisting with the integration of new members of staff

Maintaining an up-to-date working knowledge of IT systems within the firm

Attending appropriate in-house training courses

Attending performance review meetings at the appropriate time

COMMUNITY & ENVIRONMENT SERVICES
JOB DESCRIPTION AND PRINCIPAL ACCOUNTABILITIES

SAMPLE 3
COUNCIL

1 PRELIMINARIES

POST TITLE: Security Officer – as and when required

DEPARTMENT C & ES – Facilities Management

POSITION Security

2 BRIEF JOB SUMMARY

2.1 To provide support to the permanent security staff and cover for absences, as required

2.2 To provide a uniformed security service for such buildings and locations as directed to ensure the safety of employees, Members of the Council and the general public and the security of the building, its contents and its environs. Dealing with enquiries and incidents as necessary

3 MAIN DUTIES AND ACTIVITIES

3.1 Work alone or as part of a team to provide a 24 hour, 7 day a week security service for building and locations as directed by the Area Manager.

3.2 Provide an effective reception/telephone service for all callers as required outside normal office hours.

3.3 Ensure effective records are maintained in accordance with the requirements of the Service Specification.

3.4 Ensure all work is carried out in compliance with Service Specification.

3.5 Ensure compliance with all financial and administrative procedures.

3.6 Ensure all work is undertaken in accordance with the Council's Statutory Requirements and Contract Specification.

3.7 Ensure compliance with all relevant Health and Safety Legislation and the provision of a safe working environment for all members of staff, public and colleagues.

3.8 Monitor the premises fire alarm systems and intruder alarm systems and be fully conversant with emergency evacuation procedures.

3.9 Assist in evacuation of premises as required.

3.10 Provide assistance to employees, Council Members and the general public as required.

3.11 Promote, develop and maintain effective contacts and relationships with Managers, customers and Client Officers as appropriate.

3.12 Ensure that all dealings with customers are carried out in a courteous and polite manner.

3.13 Operate management systems, to enable and facilitate the delivery of services of a consistently good quality, and the monitoring and measurement of actual performance.

3.14 Undertake any other duties commensurate with the general level of responsibilities of the post.

PERSON SPECIFICATION **APPENDIX 1**

NOTES FOR APPLICANTS: This form is for you to keep. It specifies all the experience, knowledge, aptitude, skills and personal qualities necessary to perform the duties of the post for which you are applying, to the required level.

You should ensure your application explains how your experience, skills, abilities and knowledge gained in paid or unpaid work, study or training, meets each of the selection criteria marked 'A' below, including Equal Opportunities where specified.

If you fail to do so you will not be short-listed.

OFFICERS COMPLETING FORM: Facilities Manager

JOB TITLE: Security Officer – as and when required

DEPARTMENT/SECTION: Community & Environment Services – Facilities Management

CATEGORY	ESSENTIAL JOB REQUIREMENTS	METHOD OF ASSESSMENT *(See key overleaf)*
1 EQUAL OPPORTUNITY Specify objective Equal Opportunity criteria related to effective job performance.	1.1 Able to demonstrate an understanding of equality issues and commitments to the aims and objectives of the Council's Equal Opportunities Policy in employment and service delivery. 1.2 Able to deal fairly and equally with colleagues and members of the public.	I I
2 JOB-RELATED KNOWLEDGE, APTITUDE, SKILLS Identify specific job knowledge **necessary** for the effective performance of the post.	2.1 Working knowledge of alarm systems including checking and setting. 2.2 Aptitude for dealing with the public in difficult/ problem situations. 2.3 Ability to control and deal with emergency situations. 2.4 Verbal and written communication skills. Including simple written reports. 2.5 Well-developed interpersonal skills.	A I I A/I A/I
3 CUSTOMER CARE Specify what particular customer care experience is necessary relevant to this role.	3.1 Ability to provide a high standard of customer care at all times ensuring high excellence of service delivery. 3.2 Ability to work alone or as part of a team. 3.3 Excellent telephone manner. 3.4 Ability and experience in producing legible written reports.	A/I I A T
4 EXPERIENCE Specify what particular type and depth of experience are **necessary** for the effective performance of the duties. Relevant voluntary work experience should be considered.	4.1 Must be able to provide checkable employment references.	A/I

This sample is continued on following page

CATEGORY	ESSENTIAL JOB REQUIREMENTS	METHOD OF ASSESSMENT
5 EDUCATION Specify what level of qualifications (if any) is **necessary** for the effective performance of the duties.	5.1 Successful completion of secondary education.	A/I
6 PERSONAL SKILLS Specify those skills which are most relevant to effective job performance.	6.1 Honest and reliable. 6.2 Ability to deal tactfully with difficult/stressful situations. 6.3 Ability to work in high pressure and emergency situations. 6.4 Leadership skills. 6.5 Able to work on own initiative and with minimum supervision	I I I I I
7 OTHER QUALITIES (Only where relevant to effective job performance) e.g. Physical or operational requirements.	7.1 Physically able to deal/cope with potentially violent situations. 7.2 Physically fit and able to walk long distances. 7.3 High standard of personal presentation. 7.4 Able to work outside in all weather conditions. 7.5 Able to work in accordance with operational requirements and Contract Specification including 24 hour shift rota if required. 7.6 First Aid Qualification or able to attain a First Aid Certificate. 7.7 Security NVQ or other equivalent Security qualification or experience 7.8 Able to work at short notice in Felpersham	I I I A A/I A/I A/I A/I
DESIRABLE CRITERIA		
Assessment Method: A = Application Form I = Interview T = Test		

The key to using these documents effectively is to clarify the core purpose of the role and, from that, the most significant attributes that the recruiter is looking for. In all of these different layouts, the core functions of the roles are listed, together with key attributes that they are looking for. In the example of the council security officer, you even have the useful explicit instruction:

> *"You should ensure your application explains how your experience, skills, abilities and knowledge gained in paid or unpaid work, study or training, meets each of the selection criteria marked "A" below, including Equal Opportunities where specified.*
>
> ***If you fail to do so you will not be short-listed."***

This instruction is valid for every application that you make via a CV or an application form. In the housing association example (Sample 1), you have the weightings given to each of the skills and knowledge measures, which gives you a clear clue about the level of experience they are looking for.

In your live applications, you should also have supplementary research about your target organisation that builds your understanding of its values and priorities. Consider what key words you have picked up from your target website and literature about what appears to be its public image and reputation. You might find a highlighter pen helpful here to pick out the words you keep reading from all the recruitment literature. As a rule of thumb, the more frequently they appear, the more significant they are for the job. You need to ensure that the first couple of examples in your core achievements or skills list on your CV or application form demonstrates and even mentions those key words.

Even when completing an application form, you select the information that you choose to put in front of the recruiter, so your guiding principle is to find examples from your experience that suit the competences being requested. For example, you may be looking for a retailing role; we are all retail consumers to a greater or lesser degree and have our own perceptions of the big names on most high streets. Different retailers chase different markets and consequently adjust their image, advertising, language, store appearance and crucially, for the retail jobseeker, expectations of staff behaviours to suit their product range and target customers. Recruiters for an upmarket women's clothing store are looking for different customer service behaviours in their applicants from the recruiters in a swift customer throughput, bargain store. Detailed product knowledge is vital for a sales assistant in a top of the range wine store and speed at working the till is vital for the bargain shop. All of these jobs are in the same industry, but I would expect candidates to be highlighting different skills and experiences in their CVs, depending on which job they target. An HR Director once summed this up well:

> *"It seems so basic, but it never ceases to amaze me how many people – even at senior level – don't bother to do their homework properly about the companies and people they are being interviewed by. There really is no excuse for it in the age of the internet, and it makes us think, "Why should we employ you when you can't even be bothered to find out how we work?"* HR DIRECTOR

The next activity will help you to read actively the full details of any job description, person specification or other organisational literature that paints a picture of how that organisation works and what it values. Reading 'between the lines' will ensure that you use the right words and examples in your application to demonstrate the match. As you work through this exercise, also refer to your list of core competences evidence that you completed right at the beginning of the book on page 9, your first WOW map on page 21 and your Challenge, Action, Results framework on page 82. If you have already completed a core CV, then check that for the best examples to adapt for this application. This is one of those checklists that would be helpful to complete in pencil for each separate application you make, or photocopy the blank page before you start.

EXERCISE 2: Checklist for reading recruitment literature productively

I HAVE READ . . .	KEY WORDS AND THEMES	RELEVANT EXAMPLES FROM MY EXPERIENCE THAT I SHOULD HIGHLIGHT
Job description		
Person spec		
Job advert		

This exercise is continued on following page

I HAVE READ . . .	KEY WORDS AND THEMES	RELEVANT EXAMPLES FROM MY EXPERIENCE THAT I SHOULD HIGHLIGHT
Product/service/ marketing brochures		
Organisational missions statement or values		
Customer or staff newsletter		
Press releases		
Personal contacts in that organisation tell me		
Other material/ organisation's website		

■ The covering letter/email

This brief but still vital document remains relevant in the world of online recruitment and is frequently forgotten or taken for granted by many jobseekers. It should be clear and make an immediate, positive impact on the reader. When I read a strong covering letter, I am cheered by the expectation that I am about to read the CV of someone who pays attention to detail and has taken time to consider their initial impact on me. The adjective 'brief' should mean no more than three paragraphs, whether in letter or email format.

The purpose of a covering letter is to:

- Take your first opportunity to impress the recruiter.
- Summarise your interest in the role.
- Hook the recruiter's attention to read on to your CV.
- Support your application if a form hasn't enabled you to stress your key points strongly enough.
- Summarise your key matches to the role.

A helpful format to structure any covering letter is to use a similar framework to planning your networking and research emails and phone conversations that you covered in Chapter 2 on page 43. The email or letter must quickly and clearly:

- introduce yourself,
- explicitly state your key offer and how it matches what the recruiter is looking for,
- engage the recruiter's interest to read further and
- explain how you reached the organisation or where you found the advertisement.

Just as with CVs or application forms, the words must be your own. So long as you check that you are including the correct achievements in the middle paragraph, then you can probably create a core covering letter that you then adapt for each application, like using your core CV. Have a look at this example letter from Wendy, applying for an advertised vacancy and see if you think that she is achieving the core purpose of a covering letter.

27, Acacia Avenue
Felpersham
Borsetshire
BO27 8NO
Tel: 07773 567890 (mob)
Wendy@anyemail.co.uk

Date

Dear Mrs Carter,

My name is Wendy Smith, currently a part-time sales administrator in an estate agency. I wish to apply for the post of Tourism Advisor, as advertised on the Felpersham Tourist website and attach a copy of my current CV, which outlines my extensive customer service experience.

I was very excited to learn of this opportunity to join the Tourist Information Office, as I would love to share my interest in local history and landscape with our many visitors. I have been frequently praised for my attention to detail and courtesy when dealing with customers in a range of situations, including managing sensitive information. I am used to a busy, retail working environment with rapidly changing priorities and unpredictable customer needs, which I can deal with calmly and effectively.

I can offer you relevant work experience and a personal passion for promoting our beautiful local countryside to visitors. I look forward to being able to discuss my application further with you.

Yours sincerely,

Wendy Smith

TIP
Word perfect
Test your draft covering letter by reading it out loud. Can you hear energy, enthusiasm and competence? If not, you probably haven't yet nailed the right words – try some different ones.

You have just read a covering letter which introduces a CV written in response to a specific advertisement. Although you have not read the job advertisement, you should by now be able to make a pretty accurate estimate of the core competencies and experience asked for in this advertisement by reading the covering letter. Also consider the fact that you have probably been a customer of a tourism office yourself and therefore have a view on the key demands for this role. I'd suggest that a strong message jumped out from Wendy's research that the tourism office were looking for someone:

- with a track record in a face-to-face customer service role
- with experience of dealing with a wide range of customer needs
- comfortable with a fast pace of work in a busy office environment
- with knowledge of the tourism industry or an interest in some aspect of local tourism

If you guessed all of those before reading that list, then congratulations because you are now thinking like a recruiter!

CASE STUDY

How *not* to write a covering letter

Perhaps the worst covering letter I have ever seen was from an internal candidate who clearly assumed that he was entitled to an interview simply because he already worked for that organisation. The letter was literally scribbled in pencil on a sheet ripped from a lined notebook and read:

> Dear (Name of HR officer),
> I want to have an interview for the post of X. You'll find my personnel files in your office. I'm available for an interview all next week,
>
> Regards,
> Name

The letter cannot even be properly described as covering anything as it instructed the HR officer to dig out his personnel files herself. Internal job applications are tricky, (more help for you on this issue in Chapter 5 on page 176), but this candidate was clearly so far from understanding what was expected of him, that it took a very long time for the HR officer to explain why his application did not deserve an interview.

■ Managing the recruitment agencies

You may hear about very different experiences of recruitment agencies from fellow jobseekers: some have high praise and some curse agencies to high heaven. These different anecdotes are probably more to do with how the job-seekers communicated or failed to communicate with the agencies, rather than wildly different behaviours from the agencies themselves. Whatever your views of agencies, they should be forming a key plank of your job search plan as they cover just about every job role imaginable and every area of the country. The key to making the agencies work for you is to be as helpful to them as you can. In Chapter 2, page 52, there is advice on getting the best out of a recruitment agency website. Whether using their websites or their offices, you will always get a better service from them if you stay polite, visit them regularly and cultivate a relationship with one person who can get to know you well and think of you when the right vacancy pops up.

The art of managing the recruitment agency is to manage your own expectations of them. Note the business model of a recruitment agency: they find the right candidate for an organisation which does not have the time, resources, expertise or wish to publicise their vacancy. Consequently they earn their money from and consider their clients to be the organisations with vacancies, not the jobseekers they place. It is in everyone's best interests to place the right candidates with the right jobs, so please remember that you may not be their client, but you do represent their future reputation and therefore need to be happily placed. When the job market is tight and agencies have many more candidates on their books than they can place next week, you need to make your application to them stand out.

Be selective in your choice of agency rather than dropping off CVs at every door along the high street or every online agency. Many agencies specialise in certain areas, industries or job roles. Once you have completed your research in Chapter 2 to clarify what sort of job you want to target, one of the first issues to discover is which agencies specialise in that industry, job role or area. The specialist agencies have stronger contacts with your target organisations, are more up to speed than a generalist recruiter on the target industry and therefore will help you to keep updated better too.

Personal meetings will get you into a productive agency relationship quicker than a series of emails or even phone calls. Unless the market leader agency for your target role is on the other side of the country, then make the effort to meet face to face at least once. You can then establish in a formal meeting what you have to offer, what you are looking for and get their advice on how close you are to your target role. Once you have established that rapport with your friendly agency, then keep them updated at a minimum rate of at least fortnightly, preferably weekly.

Many jobseekers assume that after they have had an initial meeting with an agency recruiter, they can sit back and wait for their own personal job researcher to come up with their ideal vacancy. The truth is that every week, new, keen and shiny jobseekers are interviewed by the agencies. With the best will in the world, whenever an agency receives a commission for a particular role, they will instantly pull out all the relevant CVs of jobseekers that they have spoken to recently. As time goes by, your impressive interview performance and your unique personal experience will fade from their memory and only the most recent promising jobseekers will be put forward for that juicy vacancy. Make sure that your name is kept in front of the recruiter's memory by phoning up or dropping in regularly to keep them updated. As you do this, you will also be reinforcing the message that you are a keen and genuine jobseeker eager for a specific role and prepared to put in the time to seek it out. If they haven't heard from you for four months, they assume that you have either found another job or were simply bored and testing out what else might be on the market, i.e. not a serious jobseeker.

As a matter of courtesy, please tell them when you land a job through another route. They can neatly archive your records and will list your file as that rare example of an efficient and courteous candidate. That record might be helpful to you in another few years when you are looking for your next role. Politeness is a vital tool for anyone who wants to build their career on a series of temporary roles. Temporary agency managers tell me that when committed and reliable jobseekers build personal relationships with them, they can be offered effectively a permanent series of temporary contracts, as they give the agency repeat business from satisfied clients.

At the start of your relationship with the agency, please follow all instructions about completing their paperwork fully. It might seem a bit tedious or long-winded initially, but the more information they have about you, the better fit will be the vacancies they put you forward for. Agencies like to give everyone an initial general interview and will probably ask you to complete their application form as well as take a copy of your core CV. All the advice above about completing application forms carefully is valid here. This is all very useful development for you, as you will get some feedback from an experienced recruiter about how you interview and what sort of vacancies are most likely to be available for you now. Some will even give you some free advice on building your CV, although I can proudly say that jobseekers who I have helped are often praised by agencies for the clarity and focus of their CVs.

If they invite you to an interview with any organisation that does not result in a job offer for you, then the agency is usually given the task of delivering the news to unsuccessful candidates. Always ask for feedback from them and follow the guidelines suggested at the end of Chapter 4 on page 146. If you are not clear about the reasons for your rejection, then politely ask for clarity and please respond in a professional manner, even if you are not happy with what you hear. Understanding why the employer didn't think you were a good enough fit for this job is good, if uncomfortable, learning for you and should be able to prompt you to improve on your next application.

■ Seeking finance for self-employment

If you are considering setting up your own business as a result of your research in Chapter 2, then much of the advice given in this chapter is still valid for your business plans. The central principles of selecting the right information and presenting it clearly, positively and succinctly are the same for CVs and business plans. Your aim is to persuade someone to give you enough time to convince them that either you are the best fit for their role or that you would spend their money wisely and provide them with a good return on investment. The only difference between a CV and a business plan is the detail of content. Indeed as part of a business plan, most banks ask for your CV anyway, to help them understand your work experience to date. Consequently even if you are quite clear by now that self-employment is your target role, then you still need to generate an up-to-date CV that lists your key skills and achievements for your financial gatekeepers.

As part of your research in Chapter 2, you will have already walked up and down the high street picking up leaflets from every bank that markets loans to business start-ups. They currently offer different resources and levels of support but all want to support the next potential millionaire entrepreneur, which means **you**! If you are passionate about your business idea and present them with thorough market research that demonstrates that you understand and can describe your target potential market and are aware of how current and potential competitors could affect your growing business, then you can get the finance you need. Everyone has heard of the recent headlines about banks now being much tighter with their loans for entrepreneurs: view this as a good discipline to make your business plan as thorough as possible. Have a look at the PEST and SWOT analysis tools starting on page 59 in Chapter 2, which should provide the springboard for your loan application. Most banks will actively encourage you to include your SWOT and PEST analyses with your business application, as evidence that you have put in more work than dreaming up a coffee break idea scribbled on the back of an envelope.

Overleaf is a simple checklist that I have used with budding entrepreneurs in a range of industries. When they have completed this checklist and present it to banks as part of their loan application, they often receive positive feedback about the clarity of their business plan. It is not intended to be a full business plan but to prepare you to develop your complete business plan. As well as helping you to secure your finance, it could guide you in running your business and growing it in the future. Every business needs to regularly review their progress against clearly stated aims; this checklist will help to stop you from becoming overwhelmed by the day-to-day tasks and ensure that you are keeping in mind the big picture of where your business is going. Most banks will want you to complete their own application forms from the start. Having used this checklist as a model, you have already been prompted to think deeply about the objectives, purpose, structure and position of your business. Now you can fill in their forms with clarity and focus, and provide the detail of your intentions for their money alongside your passion for your business idea.

Have a go at working through these questions to probe your own understanding of your business plans. You might read some of these prompt questions as a little aggressive. They are designed to challenge your thinking and test whether you are wholly committed to the hard work, frustration and exhilaration that running your own business will offer you.

> *"A lot of people give up when the world seems to be against them, but that's the point when you should push a little harder. I use the analogy of running a race. It seems as though you can't carry on, but if you just get through the pain barrier, you'll see the end and be okay. Often, just around the corner is where the solution will happen."*
>
> JAMES DYSON, Designer and Entrepreneur

EXERCISE 3: Checklist for presenting a business plan for finance applications

About you:	■ What skills and experience do you currently have that suit self-employment? ■ What new skills will you need to learn to make this business successful? ■ How many hours per week can you give this business over the next three years? ■ What other commitments will need your time? How viable is your estimate above of the time you can give to the business? ■ How will you spend that time on the business? ■ What benefit will you bring to the business for that time? ■ If you got flu at any time over the next three years, what would that cost the business? What would it cost if you were ill for longer than flu? ■ Who will be your emotional support network and how will they help you? ■ Who do you know running their own business now who could advise/help you? ■ Why haven't you launched this business idea before now? ■ What risks do you face in setting up and operating this business? What level of risk is too high for you?
About your business idea:	■ Describe your business idea in one short paragraph. ■ What benefits does your business sell and to whom? ■ What is the unique selling point of your business? ■ Who are your competitors? ■ How are your services/products better than theirs? ■ How will your customers find you and understand that you have a solution to sell them? ■ What research have you done to demonstrate that there is a demand for your services/products? ■ Where will this business be in five years? ■ What are its Strengths, Weaknesses, Opportunities and Threats? *(see Chapter 2, page 63)* ■ What is the right legal structure for this business and why? (sole trader, limited company, partnership, franchise?) ■ What is the business name? Have you checked with Companies House, copyright and trademarks legislation that this name is legally available to you? ■ What image is created by the business name and other branding to date and what does your market research suggest that potential customers think of it? ■ What premises will you need to operate the business? ■ How can you use local business support networks for practical advice?

About the finance of your business:  	■ How much money are you putting into the business and what percentage is it of the total finance that you need? ■ How much money are you asking for and what will you spend it on? ■ What benefit will this money buy for the business? ■ How will you pay this loan back over the next three to five years? ■ What will it cost to produce your planned products/services? ■ What price will you sell them at? ■ What is your profit per sale? ■ What is your monthly sales target for the first three years? ■ What will be your monthly profit for the first three years? ■ What income are you planning to take out of the business over the first three years? Can the business afford that income? Can you live on that income? ■ Which additional skills will you need to buy into the business, how much will that person/people cost and how do you know that this estimate is accurate?

By this stage of your job search you now have a finely developed set of job seeking skills:

- ***You have undertaken thorough research to decide on what you want and need from the next stage of your career and you are clear about what these plans will bring you.***
- ***You have targeted your job search, which has focused your energy on delivering quality rather than quantity and enabled you to unearth the most promising employers who have the vacancies you would suit.***
- ***You have sent to the right people effective and attractive CVs and/or application forms that quickly hook their interest and can persuade them to offer you an interview.***
- ***If you want to pursue self-employment, you have put together an impressive case for financial support and can sell your business to potential backers quickly and positively.***

You are now ready to talk to a stranger about your many skills, talents and attributes and impress them at interview.

CHAPTER 4

Interview Questions & Answers

... and performing well

By the end of this chapter, you will be able to:

- ***Prepare confidently for any job interview.***
- ***Describe how the recruiter plans to manage the selection process from this point.***
- ***Rehearse all key questions asked at virtually every interview.***
- ***Tailor your answers to suit your experience and the job that you are targeting.***
- ***Practise effective answers to the toughest questions.***
- ***Manage your nerves before and during an interview.***
- ***Prepare questions to develop your understanding of your target role and impress the recruiter.***
- ***Review your interview performance objectively and learn from it.***

"Again, many thanks for your help. The questions you highlighted came up in all of my interviews so far and it's definitely comforting to keep one step ahead of the action!"

CHRIS WATKINS,
Legal Services, coached by Sian

Congratulations! You have a clear picture of what you can offer to potential employers, you have completed some solid research on current job opportunities, built yourself a sound CV and made a favourable impression on a recruiter. You have now been invited to develop your sales pitch in front of a human being who can make the decision to hire you. That's all an interview is. Inexperienced jobseekers can become very daunted at this stage, especially when the jobs market is difficult and it has taken a lot of research and effort to get as far as an interview offer. You can manage your nerves effectively and prepare to dazzle by focusing on what the recruiter looks for during an interview and offering them just that.

Once someone has made the decision to shortlist you for interview, you have already beaten most of your competitors, so the statistics are now in your favour. The number of candidates on a shortlist varies according to the response rate to the initial advert, the state of the current labour market for that role and the standard of the applicants. However, as recruitment is a very labour-intensive activity for any organisation, every shortlist will only consist of as many people as the recruiter(s) can manage in one or two days of interviewing. I have worked as a member of recruitment teams on shortlists of 25 people for one vacancy, which was a ridiculous judgement by the client, and also on a shortlist of two. As far as you are concerned, the final number of competitors on the shortlist is irrelevant; your job is to demonstrate to the recruiter that you are the best fit for their vacancy. **Remember that recruiters assess candidates for jobs against the ideal person specification, not against each other.**

At this point in the process, the recruiter's task is to get to know more about the shortlisted candidates by meeting them in person. They will ask more detailed questions about your experience and talents and enable you to find out more about the job and organisation that you claim to be interested in joining. Recruiters look for the candidate who best fits their job and person specification and can now only whittle down the potential matches by talking to all of them. Recruiters never want to waste time and money by asking 'trick' questions, trying to embarrass you or trip you up in some way. We recognise that everyone gets nervous at interview and we want to put you at your ease so that you can talk about yourself and your achievements in the most positive way possible. Consequently, all the opening small talk that you will encounter at the beginning of an interview (conversations about the weather, traffic, your journey) is just that: small talk to get you talking a little about your immediate personal experience to help settle you before we get to the main questions.

Some candidates appear more nervous than others and rarely, this nervousness can sabotage their presentation. I had a boss once who described the process as, "It's OK to be nervous, you just need to get the butterflies in the stomach flying in formation." In order to get them into formation, the nerves are best dealt with by effective preparation so that you can start the interview alert, a tiny bit anxious and simply ready to demonstrate how well you fit the vacancy.

"Nothing in life is to be feared. It is only to be understood."
MARIE CURIE, Nobel prize winner in Physics and Chemistry

■ Preparing for success

To prepare effectively, you need to consider some logistical issues to ensure that you arrive punctually at the right place, feeling quietly confident. That may sound like a very simple task to you but, on a daily basis, recruiters waste time waiting for candidates who have managed to get themselves lost or are otherwise confused about where to go and what to expect at interview. By following these tips, you will give yourself even more opportunities to research your targeted organisation and demonstrate your ability to turn up on time; a vital skill for every vacancy on the market.

As every candidate wants to know what questions they will be asked, I will also cover the most predictable questions that you will get asked at virtually every interview that you will attend and suggest some productive answers. This chapter focuses on preparation for a single recruiter interview – or, at most, two recruiters – which is the most likely interview format that you will encounter. Chapter 5 covers all other kinds of interviews, including panel interviews (three or more recruiters), assessment centres, telephone interviews, second interviews, internal interviews, informal interviews, online selection and aptitude tests.

The ideal candidate arrives calmly and approximately ten minutes early into the reception area of their target organisation. They know who to ask for at the reception/security desk by name and title, and are ready to discuss both small talk and their past achievements with a stranger. They know what to expect during the interview and approximately how long they will be there. A simple logistics checklist that everyone can use follows:

- Where is my interview?
- How long will it take me to get there?
- What is the best method of transport?
- In case of emergency (Tube strike, traffic jams, etc.), what are my alternative transport options?
- If driving, where will I park?
- Roughly how long will the interview take? (For example, part of the scheduled interview process could include a tour of the workplace.)
- Do I know exactly what to expect at the interview?
- Will they ask me to take any aptitude tests, how many people will be interviewing and who should I ask for on arrival?
- Which version of my CV did I send this organisation?
- Have I revised all the research notes that I made on this organisation and my target vacancy?
- Have I chosen and ironed the right clothes to wear?
- Which questions are they most likely to ask me?
- What shall I ask at interview?

PLAN YOUR TRAVEL ARRANGEMENTS

It is important to think ahead. I once interviewed an initially promising candidate but as the interview progressed he steadily lost attention and focused on surreptitious glances at his watch. When we reached the section of the interview inviting him to ask questions, he wanted to know how much longer the interview would take as he needed to put more money into a car park machine!

As a minimum you need to phone someone in the organisation to confirm your attendance at interview, so maximise your opportunities to impress them with your detailed research and grab the chance to ask further questions about the interview process and the job. Use the above checklist as your prompt for the phone conversation. Even if you ask questions of an administrator rather than the interviewer, they will always note your diligence and you will start the interview labelled as 'the candidate who did extra homework and sounds really keen.'

Many candidates fret over what they should wear to interview and waste a lot of energy worrying about clothes. The phrase 'business wear' is remarkably elastic when considering all possible job roles and industries that make up the modern workplace. The only rigid piece of advice I would offer is to choose something appropriate and not change your mind after you have ironed it the night before. 'Appropriate' means something that makes you look like you already hold your target job and is clean and neat; no loose threads or buttons. Sparkling cleanliness, especially fingernails, is particularly important for any role in the health or hospitality sectors or most front-line customer service roles. The old-fashioned concept of 'good grooming' is applicable to every job interview outfit; you do not need to dress in a brand-new, overtly expensive suit but please check that your shoes look clean. If you do have a trusted friend who always looks smartly turned out, you may want to ask them to advise on your interview outfit. You could choose to spend a lot of your money on the advice of a professional image consultant if you really want to. The recruiter will only actively notice what you wear if it jars with expectations of what current jobholders look like or if your clothes appear to get in the way for you because you are sitting very stiffly or fidgeting. Above all, be comfortable in order to be relaxed.

TIP

Making a fragrant impression

If you are a smoker you may have noticed a wincing or wilting interviewer when you make that initial handshake. Give your next interviewer a break and try some nicotine patches for a few days beforehand. Most recruiters have, at some time, also had to catch their breath at candidates' over-enthusiastic application of aftershave or perfume, so it is wise to limit the amount you use.

Taking time off

Arranging time off from your current workplace may be difficult or, at best, a delicate request to make. If you are currently working part time, unemployed or doing voluntary work, then recruiters would not expect you to have any problems in meeting the time and date assigned to you for interview. They do understand that it may not be possible for you to have a specific half-day or a few hours off from your current full-time employment at short notice. Recruiters are always open to the possibility of negotiating the time of interview if you are finding it hard to get the time off but they also have time pressures on them. Depending on the number of people involved in the recruitment, their location and the scale of recruitment process, they may or may not be willing to offer an alternative time. Please try to make a new appointment as close as possible to the original plan.

Once you confirm the interview time, please always book holiday from your current employer and do not be tempted to go sick for interview. You do not need to give a reason for asking for a day or half-day off and if you are successful at interview and subsequently hand in your notice, there will be a note of suspicion about your sick day hanging over your last days with your current employer. Could you concentrate on a demanding interview with part of your brain dealing with the guilt of having lied to your employer about being ill? I have heard of a woman who called in sick to go to an interview where she met a colleague who was officially on holiday and knew that she had reported being ill that morning. The cautionary tale ends with a new job offer for the holidaying interviewee and the sack for the malingering interviewee.

Waiting for your interview

A productive way to spend your ten minutes' waiting time in a reception area is to bring copies of all the notes you have made about the vacancy and this organisation, including a copy of the application form or CV that you sent them. View it as your final revision time before you start the interview. There may be product, promotional or other information available for all visitors to read in the reception area; it is always worth a glance at the latest copy of the staff newsletter to increase your understanding of the organisation. If that still sounds too stressful, then use the time as wisely by observing how colleagues greet each other or how visitors are welcomed. I always try to arrive at any client meeting a little ahead of time and watch what happens in the reception area: I find it immensely revealing of how an organisation communicates and consequently an indication of what it must feel like to work there. It is always possible that you may get a hint while you wait that this might not be the right organisation for you. That should still be regarded as a good use of your time as the purpose of an interview is for both parties to check their match.

If you are offered a cup of tea/coffee/water while you wait, then please accept if you have a dry mouth; it will help to prevent your voice sounding squeaky with nerves. No one is trying to test your manual dexterity in carrying a cup of tea, a coat, some papers or a bag, etc. and shake hands; they just want to put you at ease. Please also use your waiting time to check that your mobile is now completely off; even a silent vibrating call will distract you during the interview and you need to leave your brain clear to listen hard for the next hour or so. The recruiter would also be very grateful if you weren't too embarrassed to ask the way to the nearest toilets at this point; it is better to have a very brief delay to the interview than have you not concentrating all the way through. I would actually recommend a quick visit to the toilet, not just for comfort and nerves, but also to swiftly check that you have no spinach in your teeth or to comb your hair after a windy walk across the car park.

If deep breathing is what works for your nerves, then just sit and breathe slowly while you wait. There is huge scientific validity in the theory that deep, slow breathing calms nerves and focuses the mind; it will give your brain vital extra oxygen and contribute to getting those butterflies in formation. There is more guidance on deep breathing later in this chapter on page 140.

It is quite possible that if your interview is due to start at any point from mid morning onwards, then the process may have already overrun. Please be patient with your interview team. With the best will in the world, the most experienced interviewers can run into unexpected delays; we never want to deliberately put you under stress by asking you to arrive far too early. If you are kept waiting, cheer yourself up with the thought that one of your competitors must have arrived late and the kind recruiters are trying to ensure that even the late candidate has a fair crack at the whip by being asked all the prepared questions. The late candidate will still lose marks on the punctuality assessment and you will score highly on it.

One clear point of interview etiquette you need to know about concerns a possible overlap of candidates. If you arrive early and the day's timetable is starting to unravel, you may get to see one of your competitors being shown out before you, or you may see the next candidate waiting. If this happens to you, please do not stare; you need to focus all your brain energy on your own presentation. If you do know the other candidate, you have to make a

CASE STUDY

Stay on the wagon

On a final note about calming nerves before interviews, never drink alcohol, save it for afterwards. Some hardy souls may believe in the myth of 'Dutch courage' but it will always be noticed. I was once interviewing for a warehouse foreman and had reached the first candidate after lunch. As I opened the door to the little waiting area, a wall of whisky fumes hit me. I ran through the interview fairly swiftly, but terrifyingly, he interviewed extremely well and appeared stone-cold sober. By the end of the interview, my head was swimming. After showing him out, I opened the tiny window in the interview room, letting in winter gales and went to collect the next candidate. He walked into the room, sniffed deeply and looked at me very suspiciously. No doubt he is still telling the anecdote of the day he was interviewed by a woman who appeared to be sober, but who smelled dreadfully of whisky. No organisation will appoint anyone to a position, let alone one with so many health and safety implications, who smells of alcohol and appears to be sober.

quick decision about whether you acknowledge them or ignore them. As I was brought up to be polite to everyone, I'd recommend that a brief hello would be in order but please don't embark on a long conversation about past times or ask them what they're doing here. That answer is clear to all parties present and the subsequent conversations will only delay the recruiter's timetable further. During assessment centres a different set of protocols should be observed as you will meet and be expected to work with your direct competitors: more about assessment centres in Chapter 5, page 151.

■ Strong answers to interview questions

I guarantee that most of the following questions will be asked of you at every interview you attend between now and your retirement. You will not necessarily hear precisely these words, but the questions listed below are typical of the most common questions posed by recruiters in any industry. As you already know, the core purpose of an interview is to explore the shortlisted candidates in more detail to identify which candidate is the best fit for the vacancy. Consequently there is a small core of key questions which apply to all recruitment situations, regardless of the specific job or industry involved.

With all the suggested good practice responses given here, please do not apply them as a script, but build on them using your own words and examples that you feel comfortable with, using the work spaces provided. Recruiters can always tell which words are your own telling of your story and which have been learned by rote from someone else. When constructing your answer, the golden rule is to consider why the recruiter has asked this question and how your answer can demonstrate how well you fit the vacancy. I'd recommend that you use pencil or keep photocopying the pages with blank boxes (or use more wallpaper, *see Chapter 1, page 20*), because you should be polishing these answers and reshaping them for each separate interview that you will attend.

Once you have scribbled your own ideas into the spaces below, then practise delivering your answers either with a trusted friend or in front of a mirror to check your visual and audible impact. This really helps you if you feel nervous, or are unused to formal interviews. Practice makes you more fluent and appear more confident in what you say. There is more guidance on creating a positive impression on page 140.

The interviewer is expecting to hold a conversation with you, not interrogate you. They will expect to spend most of the interview listening to you expanding on your many solid examples of achievements that you have to offer. Some questions will probe more deeply than others. Most of the opening questions are intended to encourage you to offer as many examples as you can think of. The key thing to remember is that if you work through the suggestions below, you will offer more relevant, interesting and thought-through answers than your less hard-working competitors. The single most important principle is to **listen to the questions carefully** and give yourself time to respond; the silence always seems to be longer than it actually is and the recruiter wants you to consider your answer carefully, rather than rush yourself and get flustered.

1 *Tell me about yourself. Who are you?*

You're likely to hear this sort of question pretty early on as an invitation to open up about your experience and relevant skills. Consider it a gift to present your key selling points and expand on your analysis of how you match the vacancy. The recruiter wants to hear how you would summarise your own achievements and test whether it supports what you have already hinted at in your CV. What you choose to highlight in such an answer tells the recruiter what you think is important about you, and so indicates your priorities.

A helpful response is to give a brief summary of your career to date with one, or at the most, two, of your best achievements. You could highlight your two strongest skills, describing yourself as:

> "*an extremely effective*... insert appropriate job title here... *because I have demonstrated*... insert appropriate achievements or core skills here."

Have a look back now at:

- the work you completed in Chapter 1 on identifying your key achievements and core skills
- your 'Meeting Prince Charles Speech'
- your Challenge, Action, Results framework

These are your springboards for describing more of your achievements for the interviewer. Focus solely on the best examples to demonstrate how well you match the person specification that you are working to. This might require you perhaps to present some skills or activities from an earlier stage in your career; the date of these achievements is of less importance to the recruiter than the fact that you can demonstrate that you have that relevant experience. The exception to this rule is with technical work, where equipment and skill demands change so rapidly that you should limit your examples to contemporary practices.

Essentially a productive answer to this question that will impress the recruiter is a succinct ***summary*** of your ***relevant*** experience focusing on the essential or core skills and qualities as outlined in the vacancy specifications. Even if you are looking to change industries and so have gained that experience doing something very different, the recruiter will be impressed with your analytical skills and demonstration that you have considered all your transferable skills. Unconsciously, the recruiter will be noting that you are a candidate who is already demonstrating thorough research and so sincerely wants this job. Try noting down your ideas for this question in the box below:

2 *Why do you think this is the right job for you? What makes you the best candidate?*

Smile inwardly if you hear this question: it is your direct invitation to present your clearest summary yet of how well you fit the role. You will be very certain by now which are the most helpful talents to highlight here; it might be past experience, some particular 'soft skills' identified under the essential list on the person specification, or an example of a particular project/piece of work where you made a significant difference. A strong answer would be to offer two solid reasons for being the best candidate and pause to wait for either the next question or a request for more details about your solid reasons. If you list more than two examples, you risk losing focus and each example will be less compelling than the one before. Remember that although you will usually pick from the same pool of achievement examples for any recruiter, each interview should be prepared for separately and the key to success in this answer is to pick the most relevant examples. Note down in the box below what you think are your two best strengths to offer any employer:

3 *What do you consider to be your main strengths? What are your weaknesses?*

The strengths question can be tackled in the same way as the 'best fit' question above: offer two examples of qualities that you know from your research are in the essential criteria on the job and person specification. Choose examples for which you can also offer evidence of having made some sort of improvement, however small; remember the point made in Chapter 3, page 80 about the power of having a number to support your evidence. It is probably most impressive to give one example of something that you have already referred to in your application and one that is new to the recruiter. Have a further two examples up your sleeve in case you are asked for some more examples or more detail.

The weaknesses question can induce panic in the poorly prepared candidate and is frequently cited by interviewees as the question that creates the most stress beforehand. I like asking this question when recruiting and to some extent the delivery of this answer is as important as its content. What I am really looking for is self-knowledge: has the candidate considered what their current development needs are, or the future direction of their career – and can they demonstrate that they are aware of the key requirements of this vacancy? For example, if I was recruiting for an auditor, I would be concerned at a response like this:

> *"Well, I'm a big picture person myself really and detail is not always my strong point."*

because that answer demonstrates that they have a poor understanding of the key demands of the job.

You can turn this question to your advantage by choosing a 'helpful' example of a skill that you have been trying to develop and describe exactly what you have been doing to develop it. Please select something that clearly is not vital to carrying out this job. Perhaps our auditor would be better off suggesting something along the lines of:

> *"Well, I was struggling last year on my speed at checking the close-of-week sales figures. I asked the office manager to help me practise on a few past examples, with her timing me and offering a few short cuts across the sales lines. With a bit of intensive practice, I have now managed to increase my mental arithmetic speeds."*

Even if the interviewer asks for examples of weaknesses, plural, only offer one example and pause. I am probably one of the very few recruiters who would prompt you again for another example; most will move on to the next question. Have a go at describing some key strengths and a 'helpful' weakness in the box overleaf:

4 *Why do you want this job? Why do you want to work for us?*

Although it appears that your answer here should be a 'no-brainer', recruiters are frequently shocked by the number of candidates who, when given this direct invitation to show enthusiasm and clarity, appear lukewarm about the vacancy. Perhaps the worst answer I have heard was:

"Because my mates work here and it sounds good fun."

from a young man applying for a weekend warehouse job. My next question was to ask who his mates were and the names supplied doomed this interviewee, as they were the least productive members of the team.

Here, the recruiter wants to know how much you know about the organisation and the vacancy, which will demonstrate just how interested you really are. Many poor candidates still arrive at interview clearly struggling to understand themselves why they applied for this job, let alone capable of expressing that to the recruiter. These candidates may have written a promising CV, but have probably scattered it across every current vacancy in the local market and so reach interview without the sound research and self-knowledge that you now have.

You will be able to distinguish yourself by confidently outlining how this job fits into your longer term career plans, as it is the most logical next step in your career development. Be enthusiastic and positive, but please retain your dignity and don't swear your undying commitment to this organisation for the rest of your career. Recruiters are keen observers of insincerity. Have a go at getting your own language into this answer by using the box below:

5 *Why did you leave your last job? Why do you now want to move on from your present job?*

This question could arrive at any point during the interview or as a follow up to the previous question if the recruiter thinks that your last answer did not give a full enough picture. When you are clearly looking for your next career development move and your last organisation was genuinely unable to offer it in their workload or staffing structure, everyone recognises that the time had come for you to look elsewhere for your next challenge.

When you want to leave or have just left your last job for any other reason, you need to have a coherent, truthful and rehearsed answer ready. Many candidates who have been made redundant from their last job become nervous about mentioning it, even though you will have noted this on your CV to show when you last worked. Recruiters are familiar with the pressures of redundancy: many of us have also had to make people redundant, so we understand that the job rather than the jobholder has to be made redundant. It is nothing to be ashamed of. You may find it helpful to clarify in your answer the scale of redundancies, for example:

> *"There were 30 of us carrying out that role but lower demands for the service meant that only three positions were available in the new structure – and unfortunately most of my colleagues had more experience of that job than me."*

If you have not been in paid employment for some time, a predictable follow-up question to your answer might be, ***"So how have you been spending the last few months?"*** In Chapter 3, page 75, you read about the benefits of having an example of voluntary work to talk about. You will have mentioned this on your CV, but this is your opportunity to expand on which skills you are developing and why you chose to volunteer for that particular organisation.

If, for whatever reason, you parted with your last employer on poor terms, (were sacked, asked to resign or chose to leave a difficult situation) you need to practise your answer to this one very carefully. If you still feel very angry about how you were treated by your last organisation, then draft and re-draft an answer many times over until you have something that reflects your language, describes the key facts of the story and retains dignity for everyone involved, particularly you. Please follow two golden rules; tell the truth and stay diplomatic, regardless of your emotions. Some labour markets have high levels of information exchange (recruiters call it networking!) and you never know if your recruiter may know your previous boss.

It might be helpful to show your draft to a trusted friend, never someone from your close family, for their reactions. You do not need to explain every gory detail; the recruiter is genuinely interested in why you left your previous job and wants to find out how you see this vacancy as your next logical career move. They will be reassured by an answer that acknowledges that you might have made a mistake in a past role but are clear about what you did to contribute to any problem and how to avoid it happening again. As you deliver your reason for leaving, keep it brief and factual and just stop talking when you reach the end of it. This sounds so much more confident and honest than wittering on in an embarrassed manner.

If you have been in prison, there is a specific set of rules about disclosing certain offences under the Rehabilitation of Offenders Act, please refer to the brief guide to the law on page 198 for more detail. Good practice recruiters recognise that past problems need not follow candidates into their future careers. Use this box to draft your statement describing your reason for leaving.

6 *How do you perform or react under pressure or in a crisis?*

This Is not a trick question, but another attempt by the recruiter to find out how much you know about yourself and your target job. One person's crisis is the next person's bad hair day, so please choose a relevant example. Every job produces its unique stress points that need to be dealt with regularly by the jobholder, so this is a pretty common question for a recruiter to investigate your perception of 'a crisis'. A sound response would be to identify a behaviour that would not feature highly in the vacancy's specifications and honestly reflects the sort of work situations that you find difficult; have a look at the areas that you pulled out for your 'weakness' practice earlier. For example, when I recruited for a telephone customer service role dealing with complaints, I did not appoint the

candidate who cheerfully admitted that she hated people getting cross with her as it flustered her, despite having worked in a customer service role before. She got full marks for honesty but not a job offer as her answer suggested she would have found a key requirement of the role very difficult.

When answering this one, it would be really helpful if you could give an example of something that you have done to attempt to develop your resistance to this stress trigger. Another useful tactic is to be clear about what it was that you did to resolve or improve the situation; try hearing and answering the question as "How **well** do you react under pressure?" Whatever example you give, the fact that you have an appropriate example and can discuss it without embarrassment, puts you ahead of many candidates who either have never given their stress triggers a moment's thought or try to pretend that they have none at all, which is patently not true. The entire purpose of this book is to enable you to target the jobs that suit you: your experience to date, your unique skills and talents and future career aspirations. By now you know that you should be honestly assessing all your skills and capabilities to ensure that you accept the right job, not just any job. Have a go below at identifying what pressure means to you and how you react to it:

____

____

____

____

____

____

____

____

7 *In your CV, you mention that you're a good team player/very creative/flexible/good at working on your own initiative, etc... Can you give me an example of when you last demonstrated this quality?*

This question might well be repeated several times over with a variety of key competences. This is your invitation to expand on your CV and give a detailed example of how good you are at the specified competence. Here is where your preparation for building your CV comes into good use.

Instead of completing a grid for practising these answers, just use blank sheets of paper every time you prepare for an interview. Take each of the essential person specification criteria for this vacancy in turn and write out an example from your experience that demonstrates it. This will give you a secure anecdote to offer for this question, relating to any of the key criteria that your recruiter needs evidence for. For extra practice, look back to Chapter 1, page 9, Exercise 1 and work through the entire list of common competences, constructing your own personal example for each one, just in case the recruiter asks for a competence that you hadn't predicted. Do not fret if your best example comes from a different context to the work that you are currently applying for, or even from outside the world of paid employment. Most recruiters will be impressed that you can demonstrate how transferable you consider your skills and experiences to be.

Note that this question is phrased to stress recent examples: "when you **last** demonstrated this competence". If you hear this strong steer for recency, then try to pick examples of work that you have done within the last six to twelve months, depending on the competency that you are giving evidence of. Recruiters tend to prefer hearing about your more recent experience, which might prove difficult if you are trying to focus on skills gained from earlier roles. If you are pressed for more recent examples, then you have to stay honest and state that you haven't done this sort of work for X months. Without pausing, continue your next sentence along the lines of:

> *"However, I do have experience of handling customer complaints only nine months ago, when working in a different role."*

You must be ready with a strong example of another core competence that is from more recent transferable experience.

A common error for many candidates when presenting their evidence of matching the required competencies is to forget to specify their own personal contribution to a success. I often hear the phrase, "We did this and than we did that," in response to describing evidence for a particular competence and sometimes I have to prompt candidates to use the word 'I' instead. This can really fluster the candidate who has clearly never considered the simple question: what did ***you*** do to make a difference?

8 *What was the most rewarding or enjoyable part of your last job? Which achievement are you most proud of?*

Here is another wonderful opportunity for you to demonstrate enthusiasm and energy and frankly show off about what you have achieved for your last organisation. This answer needs your most impressive example and hopefully it will also solidly demonstrate the key competences needed for this vacancy. It is fine to talk about something that you may already have mentioned, so long as you can add a level of detail or demonstrate an additional skill that you haven't talked about before. Try to define your best achievement in your words below:

____

____

____

____

____

____

____

____

9 *What has been your biggest problem that you've had to manage? What has been the biggest disappointment so far in your career?*

This is not an attempt to encourage you to bare your soul or wallow in self-pity but calmly talk about any situation that you genuinely found difficult to deal with. With this question, the recruiter is looking for your view of significant stress or barriers to achievement and how you reacted to them. Your answer will reveal your definition of stress; what is important to you at work in terms of your tasks, values, skills and colleague relationships; how you respond to challenges; and what you did to try to improve the situation or limit the damage. A helpful example to consider would support the rule of matching the core target competences by identifying a problem that you overcame through applying a core competence needed for this vacancy. Be truthful, brief and focus as much as possible on what you did to remedy the issue. If any part of your problem relates to the core competences for the vacancy, check that you are minimising the unhelpful references and maximising the helpful ones. Have a go at drafting your 'significant difficulty' story in this box:

10 *If you had your time over again, what would you do differently? Have you got any examples of work that you now think was a mistake?*

This question can fluster the poorly prepared candidate, as it appears to lead you into confessing that you have done something wrong. The recruiter is looking for evidence that you understand what your key achievements and mistakes are and can demonstrate that you can learn from them.

Try to identify an example that focuses on you learning to change something about your own behaviour. Using the Challenge, Action, Result framework, simply describe what happened, what you could have done differently in order to improve the situation and specify what you have done since to ensure that it won't happen again. The example you choose shouldn't be dramatic or large scale to help maintain your air of rarely making mistakes. No one has an entirely perfect career and we all recognise situations where we vow to do or say something differently next time: it is called learning and will be a core demand from every one of your future employers, regardless of what job you will be doing for them.

Adapt the Challenge, Action, Result framework to:

Challenge: describe the problem

Action: describe what you did to contribute to the problem **and** what you did to retrieve it

Result: describe what happened and

Remedy: specify what you learned from the experience and how you are going to ensure that it does not happen again.

IDENTIFYING HOW I'VE LEARNED FROM MY MISTAKES

Challenge

Action

Result and Remedy

11 *Where do you see yourself in five years time? What is the next step in your career plans or what are your long-term career aims?*

If you hear the "Where do you see yourself in five years?" question, please do not reply, "Doing your job" or even hint at smirking. We've all heard that answer from nervous and ill-prepared candidates too many times to consider it remotely witty. Recruiters are genuinely interested in how you see your career developing and want to test out if you have thought through how relevant your current application is to your long-term plan. We want to hear from you a logical explanation of how you connect your past experience to the vacancy and your understanding of the longer-term picture for the organisation. As with many of the answers I have suggested in this section, there isn't a 'right' answer to this question, so long as you demonstrate that you have considered the issue and you know why you want this particular job. Clearly your answer to this question also develops throughout your career as you learn new skills and want to apply them in different areas.

You may be concerned, particularly when the jobs market is tough, that a prospective employer might consider you to be 'over-qualified'. Certainly I have heard recruiters use the phrase and apply it as a contributory factor for rejecting a candidate, believing that they would leave the organisation as soon as a more significant role becomes available and will therefore not show long-term commitment. Focus on the fact that you have been offered an interview as a result of your impressive initial application and consequently the recruiter is fully aware of the key highlights of your experience and all your current qualifications. They still think that you are worth talking to further, knowing that you may be considered 'overqualified' for the role. What is of more interest to the recruiter is how you see your career developing through this vacancy and what you want to learn from your future jobs. I have heard a wide variety of genuine and coherently presented reasons for moving a career in an unexpected direction from apparently 'overqualified' candidates. I am proud of having appointed several of them to posts that became very fulfilling for them and their employers. Go back to look at your work in Chapter 1, Exercise 2, page 14, on the issues that matter to you and what you are looking for from your future career. Next, draft a response in the box overleaf that describes your vision for your career starting from the vacancy that you are about to be interviewed for:

12 *What motivates you? What are the most important factors you need in a job?*

With this question, the recruiter wants to know what makes you tick and what inspires you to give of your best at work. Money may be the answer that first pops into your head but consider what the best candidate for the job would suggest. From your work in Chapter 1, Exercise 2, page 14, you have already identified the unique set of work conditions that you know enable you to give of your best at work. Some people thrive on pressure, busyness and tight schedules; others are inspired by collaborative working and seeing how their contribution makes a difference to the team effort. Some are motivated to deliver the best possible customer service, while others enjoy the thrill of closing a deal. Pick out about four highlights from your work on Exercise 2 that offer the best match possible into the core competences for your target vacancy. You should be truthful in offering the real you and focused on demonstrating what you have to offer your prospective employer. If the recruiter hears factors that correspond directly to the key requirements of the vacancy, they know that you have high potential to perform well in this role because it offers you precisely the motivating factors that you look for. Try defining your key motivators in the box below, concentrating on those that the job will directly provide:

13 *Why should we employ you? What can you bring to the job?*

If this question is phrased using the first example, it can sound rather abrupt or even intimidating: I always prefer to use the second set of words. You are likely to encounter this question either very early or perhaps more frequently, towards the end of the interview. If it appears quite late for you, keep focused to ensure that you don't simply repeat earlier answers. Clearly the recruiter is handing you another opportunity to summarise your key selling points. There is nothing wrong in repetition of your core message but the recruiter also needs to hear something new in the example or level of detail that you offer here. If you have picked up any clues from reactions, comments or questions during the interview that you might have missed the opportunity to fully sell a key competence, then respond with the right example. Use your summary statement from your CV as your start point for this answer, remember your 'Meeting Prince Charles Speech', review your draft answer to your 'best achievement' question on page 126 and create a single sentence to close your sale. The more succinct and clear your answer now, the more powerful your response will sound.

14 *What have you learned or what's the most important thing you have learned from your last job or last boss or last mistake?*

The best answer that a recruiter could hear to this question is a clear and focused description of a significant piece of learning, especially if it relates to a core competence for this vacancy. This is another question where the content is less important than the fact that you demonstrate that you are capable of learning. Every job role demands the ability to learn new skills, tasks or apply current knowledge to new circumstances. The ability to learn and identify what you have learned and how will be a central demand for every job that you hold until you retire, hence the significance of this question.

If the question is phrased as "What did you learn from your last boss?", please don't answer, "How not to do something." Even if the statement is true, then it comes across as at best ungracious and at worst, rude. Reflect on how this appears to the recruiter: if you are prepared to talk in such terms to a complete stranger about your current colleagues, they will be considering how loyal you may or may not prove to be in the future.

Try drafting an answer in the box below that offers you the opportunity to reflect on how, as well as what, you learned in recent work. If your mind is a complete blank, then start with the core competences for the role you are about to be interviewed for and ask yourself, "How did I learn to apply those competences well?"

15 *Technical Questions*

Whatever job role you apply for, you are likely to be asked some technical questions designed to check that you have the appropriate levels of skills, understanding and knowledge to carry out the role. Having completed your thorough research about the role and organisation, you will be ready for those questions. They may well be delivered along the lines of solving a hypothetical problem:

So, what would you do if . . . (a problem is outlined that has several possible next steps)

Some very technical questions will have one right answer, but most will be less clear cut and are designed to prompt you to consider a range of possibilities. It would be quite acceptable to hedge your bets so long as you explain how your thinking works, for example:

> *"If the customer's records showed me X, then I would go for Option A, but if I couldn't access that information at that time, I would go for Option B."*

Take your time on these answers: always ask for more information or the question to be repeated if something that the recruiter described did not make sense to you. If the recruiter judges the technical knowledge tests to be very important for assessing all the shortlisted candidates, then they may arrange a separate aptitude test as part of your interview schedule and you will see more notes on dealing with these in the next chapter.

A common technical question about your current knowledge could be:

> ***What training have you undertaken recently? How do you keep up to date in our industry?***

You are possibly more likely to be asked this question if you are trying to change industry, so have little or no experience – or perhaps if you are trying to return to the sort of work that you did earlier in your career. The recruiter wants to find out how much you know about the current 'hot topics' in your target job area. An alternative way of testing how much you know about the relevant hot topics is to ask your opinion directly:

> ***What do you think of the new professional standards or recent changes to industry regulations or the new widgets produced by our rivals?***

Every industry has a professional or trade organisation, usually linked to a website with some degree of public access to attract new entrants. If you are targeting a job where you currently have little experience or are working towards professional qualifications, then there is likely to be an arrangement for some sort of associate membership. As referred to in Chapter 2, page 51, professional organisations are a rich source of current knowledge about industry issues overall, as well as potential job opportunities. To maintain credibility in the interview, particularly if you are starting from a position of little relevant experience, you must be able to express an informed opinion on current key industry issues. Use the box below to practise a range of possible answers to technical questions:

16 *Have you got any questions that you would like to ask?*

This is your signal that the interview has reached its closing stages and the recruiter is handing the questions over to you. Poorly prepared candidates often appear completely panicked at this point, as they never viewed the interview as their chance to find out more about the job or the organisation. Please think of many as possible in your practice box below, but I'll focus first on what the recruiter does **not** want to hear now. If you ask a question where the answer has already been provided to you either in information sent to you about the job, or during the interview, the recruiter will start to question your ability to retain information. It is, however, perfectly acceptable to ask a more detailed question about an issue that has been referred to briefly before, if you want to explore it further. Do not start asking about the salary or benefits package attached to the job unless you are specifically invited to by the recruiter: conversations or negotiations about how much the job pays are appropriate only after you have been offered the job, which usually happens in a phone call later. (Have a look at Chapter 5, page 172 for some more help on this one.)

Helpful questions to ask at this point are any about the future of the organisation that include you in it, for example:

- How do you see this job/department/company developing over the next few years and what sort of training do you think your staff will need over that time frame?
- What do you see as the biggest opportunities/challenges for this job/department/organisation over the next year?
- How do you plan to measure the success of this role?
- What do you think are the most urgent priorities for this job?
- What are the resources allocated to this role (budget, staffing, equipment, etc.)?
- How do you see my skills and experiences fitting into your organisation?

Depending on how tired you are, how cheeky you feel and how tired your recruiter looks, it's worth requesting a brief tour of the site or asking to meet a few potential colleagues if that hasn't yet been offered to you.

You must leave the interview clear about what happens next in terms of timescales and notifying successful candidates. The recruiter will probably tell you in the closing remarks, but check it before you formally leave. Be prepared to wait a few days or even a couple of weeks if a lengthy interview process is required. It is possible that your next stage is a second interview with different people and there are a more hints on managing second interviews in the next chapter. Have a go at identifying as many positive questions for your recruiter as you can in the box overleaf. If you have had all of your prepared questions answered during the interview and cannot think of another one, then tell the recruiter so and ask for a number that you may ring later that day or tomorrow if any more pop into your head.

All that remains for you to do now is to close the interview strongly and politely.

■ Creating the right impression

So far, you have been concentrating on what to say at the interview; the most successful candidates have also considered how they say it. Reflect for a moment on the words you would like the interviewer to use in describing you. Would you like to be described as confident, friendly, professional, knowledgeable, approachable, positive, capable, enthusiastic, or any other word? Whichever attractive adjectives you would like to be used to describe you, you have control over the impression you make on the recruiter and therefore the adjectives they use to sum up their impressions of you afterwards. In order to direct these impressions, you must be clear what each of those adjectives looks and sounds like for you.

Some famous experiments were carried out in the United States 30–40 years ago to explore how people communicate when conversing. If you want to impress your friends, you could drop the name of Alfred Meerhabian into the conversation. He recorded thousands of hours of conversations, often between strangers, then separately interviewed the conversers afterwards to identify what they thought of the people they had just met and what they remembered of the conversation. A consistent message built up about how humans create their perceptions of others that provides an insight into how we all invent our own prejudices and look to reinforce them. The conclusions drawn were that the words spoken during a conversation have little bearing on your memory of how the conversation progressed and certainly don't feature much as evidence for you liking or disliking that person. Meerhabian suggested that:

- as little as 7% of our message is transmitted by the words we use
- 38% comes from the tone of voice in which those words are delivered and
- a whopping 55% of our impact on others is created by what we look like: body language, stance, movement or posture, facial expressions, clothes worn.

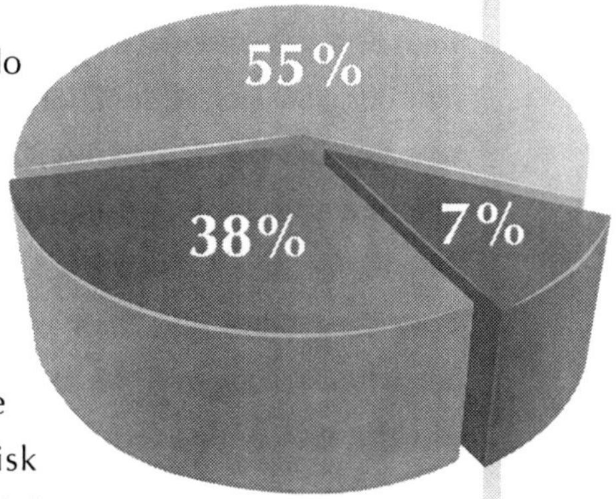

Now as a prospective interviewee, please do not become downhearted by this revelation. Recruiters are very well aware of the potential impact of what we refer to as 'the halo or horns effect' and so structure interviews and note-taking carefully to actively prevent our prejudices interfering with our evidence collection. We know that there may be a risk of pre-judging a candidate after having read their CV but before meeting them: the 'halo or horns effect', which means we risk looking for evidence during interview that merely confirms our first impressions. Because we are aware of that risk, we work as objectively as possible to ask candidates for relevant evidence of having displayed specific competences and this is why when you are interviewed by a solo recruiter, they need time to note down your responses. Solo recruiters are much rarer than two people interviewing. Recruitment decisions are so expensive that they must be made on the basis of evidence, not memory.

The implication for the well-prepared candidate is that you consider carefully your overall impact as well as rehearsing your prepared answers. You have control over the impact you create with the interviewer: you need to consider all the different ways that we communicate, not just the words that we use and listen to. By becoming more aware of the largely unconscious signals that you transmit during any conversation with another human being about your feelings and current state of mind, you will be more aware of the impact you create on that person. This is the reason for asking you to practise your delivery of your answers out loud, preferably with your trusted friend who could give you feedback on how your tone of voice, posture, facial expression, gestures, mannerisms and clothes are helping or hindering your impact.

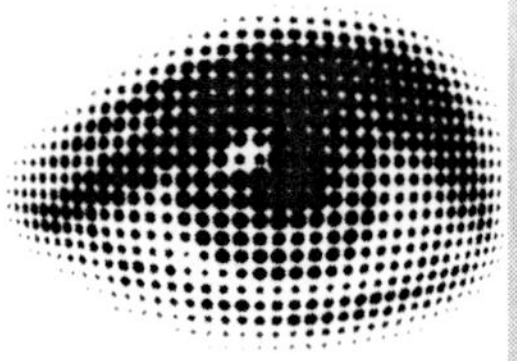

You need to be clear about what 'professional' looks like and sounds like for you. Although there are some general principles, such as a strong smile, straight stance and slower than typical speaking pace, you need help from a friend to ensure that you do not come across as a grinning, manic puppet, which is always possible for the most nervous. Eye contact is possibly the most significant message to send correctly during a potentially stressful conversation such as a job interview. Too much could leave an aggressive impression, too little suggests lack of confidence in yourself or the interview situation. Defining how much is the right amount is very hard as it varies between individuals and different cultures judge appropriate eye contact to be very different amounts. Essentially the interviewer's summary of your personal impact will be formed from their notes and their memories of your total verbal, vocal and visual behaviour throughout the meeting. Smiles and direct eye contact are seen as friendly, welcoming and open. One of the most important of many things to remember when being interviewed is to keep smiling. Have a go in the box opposite at defining your desired adjectives and the behaviours that you show when you demonstrate them. An example for 'confident' is given to start you off.

Nervousness

Considering your whole visual and audible impact is also helpful for banishing the effect of nerves. Nervousness has its own behaviour patterns too: of tight body posture, cramped movements, higher than typical voice from tightly held neck muscles and over-fast breathing, strained facial expressions and fidgeting. It might be helpful for you to identify what nervous looks like and sounds like for you, to remind you which behaviours to avoid. The single most helpful physical behaviour to control nerves, as demonstrated by generations of performers and athletes, is to focus on slowing and deepening your breathing. Straighten your back, (whether sitting or standing), drop your shoulders to

EXERCISE 1: Creating the right impression

Preferred impression	**Description of how I look and sound when I demonstrate this adjective** (tone of voice, posture, facial expression, gestures, mannerisms, clothes)
(Example) Confident	Voice slightly lower and deeper than usual, smiling, making the right amount of eye contact, taking the time to think through answers, relaxed and open sitting position

open up your chest and start to slow your outgoing breath. It brings down your heart rate and crucially gets more oxygen to your brain, which is exactly where you need it to concentrate during interviews.

Connecting with the recruiter

Remember that the interviewer is sending you non-verbal communication too, if you feel you can spare a bit of your hard working brain to consider it. When you have a 'gut feeling' about meeting a stranger and believe that something about your meeting 'clicked' so that you got on very well, then this is visual impact at work. You may notice that the recruiter will also be smiling and nodding and listening very hard to what you say: it is always in our interests to try to establish a rapport with each candidate in order to get the best out of them, except when they have clearly spent all lunchtime downing whisky!

It remains a fact of life, however, that you will find it easier to establish that rapport with some people than others. As mentioned above, recruiters are aware of this and actively work to put aside any potential lack of connection in order to assess each candidate fairly; we don't have to actually like the best candidate for the job, we just have to uncover who they are. Particularly in larger organisations, you will most likely be interviewed by a HR professional and if you apply for a job through agencies, you will have a first interview with agency staff: none of these people will end up working with you. In smaller companies or in second stage or technical interviews, you are more likely to be interviewed by your potential new boss and then it is most encouraging to feel that you are connecting with your recruiter and developing a rapport.

As well as your verbal and visual impact, please consider your behaviour towards everyone you meet at your target organisation. From the moment you walk into the building, everyone with whom you come into contact needs to be impressed by your politeness and poise. Some organisations invite their security or reception staff to contribute their comments on the candidate behaviours they saw. When you are introduced to someone, they will offer their hand and their name. Just shake their hand, make eye contact, remember to smile and if you are bothered by the fear of forgetting their name, it can help to simply repeat it, for example, "Pleased to meet you Helen." Small comments, like just murmuring, "Thanks" as doors are opened for you, will build an impression of politeness. It may be hard to believe but recruiters do come across candidates who appear incapable of any responses beyond grunts during initial introductions and walk to the interview room. We give them the benefit of the doubt though and assume that nerves render them incapable of saying thank you.

The interview room

When you reach the interview room, you will be offered somewhere to sit, please wait to be invited to sit down. I have interviewed candidates who settled themselves in front of my notes at the start of the interview and having to shuffle seats or papers makes a clumsy start. We have already covered the need for small talk before starting on the main questions. Like most recruiters, I outline for the candidate the shape of the interview, just to set both of us up about the order of events. So you could expect the interviewer to first say something like:

> *"I'm going to start by asking you a few questions about some points you made on your CV, then I'd like to explore some of your earlier experience, then I want you to have the opportunity to ask any questions you may want to. Once my bit is finished, I'm going to hand you over to Lorraine, who will set you up with a brief typing test and then offer you a quick tour of the site and the chance to meet a few more members of the team."*

I also explain about my need to take notes to re-assure the candidate that pauses between their answer and my next question are solely to make sure I am capturing accurate information.

The invitation for you to ask your own questions is a clear signal that the recruiter has finished asking all of theirs, but is not the point when you can stop listening. Concentrating hard during an interview does prove tiring, but you must stay focused until you have left the building. You can expect to close the interview with the recruiter explaining the timetable about what happens next; please ask about these details if you haven't heard them by the time you are being shown out. As you leave, expect another formal greeting and handshake at the reception desk and please take the time to leave a strong last impression. Often, the nervous candidates are so relieved at having reached the end of their ordeal that they gabble a goodbye and rush out.

As part of your leave taking, thank the interviewer for giving the time to meet you and send a brief message that you are still very keen on the job, **if that is**

still the case. You may attend an interview where, despite your best research beforehand, you learn more details about the job and/or the organisation that suggest that this is not actually the right job for you. Assuming that you are still very keen, leave the interviewer with another firm handshake, your best positive manner and a sentence along the lines of:

"I've really enjoyed learning more about Company X today and feel certain that this job is a great next step for me, thank you for your time today."

Try out a sentence for your closing comment that sounds right for you in the box below:

■ After the interview

Congratulations; you deserve a relaxing wind down, whether that means for you a cup of tea with your best friend to talk about how you feel it went, or a long walk with the dog. When you have reached home, you will discover that you will probably need an early night; listening and concentrating so intently takes it out of you. Take some time the following day, **no later than 24 hours after the interview**, to review how you think the interview went and if your helpful friend can also spare you the time, then please include them in the review.

The benefit of reviewing what is now history, is to learn for the future. If you have worked hard enough to be offered this job, this may be your last job interview for some time or you may be asked to attend a second interview, (more about second interviews in Chapter 5, page 171), or you may need to continue your efforts to secure more interviews shortly. Whatever the result, you need to gather feedback from as many sources as possible and so deliver an even better performance next time.

Keep your review simple and brief, it is of tremendous help to jot something down so that you have some notes to look at for your next interview. When I work with jobseekers reviewing their performance, we find the following questions very powerful:

- What went well for me and why?
- What did I find most difficult and why?
- If I had the same interview over again, what would I do differently and why?

An honest response to these three questions will prepare you well for all future interviews.

If you truly made a hash of something, don't beat yourself up about it, just work out what you would do differently next time. Nobody ever makes the wrong decision deliberately, so it is a complete waste of your energy to get cross with yourself. The best way to make amends is to be clear about how to ensure that you never make the same mistake twice. **It would also be very difficult for anyone who has put into practice all the advice you have read so far to still get it very wrong.**

If you suddenly think of a cracking question that you could have asked at the end but wasn't in your head at the time, then take some more deep breaths, find a quiet spot and phone your recruiter to ask the question. Be prepared for them not to be available but book a firm time through a colleague for ringing them back. When you speak to them directly, be brief, introduce yourself clearly and quickly to jog their memory (they may have interviewed half a dozen more candidates since they last spoke to you) and ask your question. If you felt that you managed to establish a good rapport yesterday, then engage your recruiter in a short conversation as appropriate and clearly say thank you again for the opportunity of the interview. You never know where a second opportunity for a conversation may take you.

Despite your best efforts, not every interview you attend will result in a job offer, as someone else may actually be a better fit to the vacancy. When the answer to all your efforts is no, it can be hard news to accept, particularly if you attended a second interview or know that you were one of the final two candidates. **The very tough golden rule for the well-prepared candidate is to always to seek feedback when the answer is no**. It may not be easy to listen to, but if you ask for feedback and listen to it carefully, then you will maximise your learning from the experience. Recruiters are willing to give unsuccessful candidates feedback and it may cheer you a little to know that we don't find it an easy task either.

It is perfectly acceptable to arrange to ring the interviewer after you receive the bad news; do not expect feedback in a speculative call as the recruiter will also want to prepare and revise all their interview notes. Be ready for a quiet and private phone call, have pen and paper for notes and an open mind. Your role during this call is to simply listen and only ask a question for clarification if you hear something that you don't understand. Be prepared not to like or even agree with what you hear. Never get defensive or try to re-present your version of events, however wrong you think their opinion is. Just swallow hard and remember to say thank you for their time and feedback. Recruiters genuinely wish candidates well and want to help them succeed in their job search, and perhaps use the call as a chance to suggest more appropriate vacancies to be chasing. It will be helpful to remember that we will always have more experience of interviews than you, so there is merit in our opinion. Most unsuccessful candidates who I speak to are very gracious about and grateful for their feedback, even though it is effectively bad news. Those who consider it when making their next application always find it a helpful development tool.

I have seen a few examples of such a positive response to the 'near miss', that unsuccessful candidates have been invited to apply for similar vacancies a few months later and actually be offered posts at their second attempt. Large organisations in particular do keep details of candidates who made a good impression at interview, if not quite good enough for appointment on their first application. It could be that a positive response to your interview feedback rewards you with the offer of a second interview.

There is more help on how to deal with this delicate situation of second interviews and other types of selection processes in the next chapter.

CHAPTER 5

Different kinds of interviews

By the end of this chapter, you will be able to prepare effectively for a strong performance in a wide range of selection processes, including:

- ***aptitude tests***
- ***assessment centres,*** *including presentations, team-building exercises, decision making/prioritising exercises, data analysis, role plays and managing the whole process professionally*
- ***informal interviews***
- ***internal interviews***
- ***online selection processes***
- ***panel interviews***
- ***psychological tests***
- ***second interviews***
- ***telephone interviews***

If you are taking a 'pick-and-mix' approach to reading this book by concentrating on the sections that are of greatest use to you, then please do not start here. This chapter really should be read as a follow-up to Chapter 4, as every piece of advice about good preparation for a standard one or two recruiter interview, also applies to preparing for any other type of selection test. This chapter covers additional selection techniques that you may encounter. It also explains the thinking behind a recruiter choosing these sorts of procedures and ensures that you will deliver of your best if you are invited to undertake any of these selection tasks. If you have never experienced anything other than a one or two person interview, then some of the processes that I describe may sound a bit daunting. Once you have worked through this chapter, you will be able to prepare effectively and understand fully what represents good performance at these sorts of recruitment processes. So, if you have not already done so, please turn to the start of Chapter 4 now and once you have read that, then return to the next paragraph.

Welcome back! Remember the hint in Chapter 4, page 111 about ensuring that you understand exactly what will be required of you during the whole selection process. Consequently, you now know how much time you expect to be spending at your interview. You have also clarified what tasks might be laid out for you in addition to an interview with one or two recruiters. The essential question remains: why do recruiters sometimes add different sorts of tests to the selection pot?

The answer is that one interview that collects evidence of applicants' past experience, current levels of knowledge, skills, attitudes and abilities does not always give a full picture of precisely what each candidate is capable of. Recruitment is a time-consuming process and therefore directly costly to organisations, so we don't flippantly add extra assessments. We need to be certain that it will help to give us better quality information about which of our candidates are closest to the ideal person specification.

Look back to page 93 in Chapter 3 at the person specification example for the Council security officer – the one that lists how the recruiter intends to assess each required competence. Most of these categories are tested by interview; some on the evidence provided by the application form; and one competence, 'Ability and experience in producing legible written reports', is to be assessed through a test. If you were preparing to be interviewed for that job, then this is a clear hint that at some point during your selection meeting, you will be asked to write a brief report. As the competence requires it to be 'legible', then you will be expected to hand write it. If I was recruiting for this post, I would prepare a brief account of a situation that the security officers might typically deal with, set up a private room and give each candidate a finite amount of time in which to write up the fictional report. As I am a kindly recruiter, I would try to set up a timetable whereby each candidate took the test after their interview, so that they would feel that their major hurdle was behind them by the time we ask them to write the report. In order to assess which of our interviewed applicants best fits the post, the recruitment team then assembles all the evidence from the candidates, which includes:

- our records of their interview answers and interview questions,
- their written reports and
- their application forms.

As all those competences are listed as essential on that person specification, we assume that it includes the ability to write legible reports. This means that even if a candidate interviewed very strongly but was not able to complete a legible and coherent brief report in the time that would be expected of an average performer, then we should rule out that candidate.

This is an example of why recruiters often need to set up additional selection tests beyond an interview. If we selected solely on interview performance and then provided the council with a security officer who couldn't summarise key points swiftly and legibly, we would be putting a square peg into a round hole. The fundamental responsibility of the recruiter is to be 100 per cent certain that all selection tests add value to the process and genuinely reflect the daily requirements of the job role. For example, if technology moved on and all the council security staff were expected to provide reports by typing on mobile devices or using voice recorders, then the need for legible handwriting would disappear from the job's essential requirements. I would still want to set a separate report-writing test though; to assess how well candidates can summarise and present key information. I would ask them to complete it on whatever equipment the current jobholders use to write their reports.

■ Aptitude tests

What I have just described is often referred to as an aptitude test. Aptitude tests vary tremendously in their format, structure, length and content, depending on what the recruiter needs to know about an essential competence for that role. Other examples of aptitude tests include typing speed tests, colour blindness tests, psychological questionnaires (more detail on these later), data analysis, driving demonstrations or handling of technical equipment, hand/eye co-ordination tasks measured by computer screen exercises, role-play scenarios to demonstrate customer service skills, prioritisation exercises to judge your ability to handle rapidly changing situations, translation exercises, presentations, meeting role-plays (often used at assessment centres, *see opposite*) numeracy, verbal reasoning, spatial ability or letter writing tests and so on.

The list is huge because the range of potential skills and competences to be tested is huge. Some examples in the list above may have surprised you, but consider the key requirements for any role. The following are examples of situations where tests might be required:

- The colour blindness test: a technical role requiring you to always identify wiring colours accurately cannot be guaranteed to be safe if a red/green colour blind person performs that job.
- It is now common practice when recruiting in schools for any teacher, whether newly qualified or experienced, to be asked to prepare and deliver a brief lesson to a group of children that will be observed by the recruiting team.
- If my company has urgent need of a forklift driver and no capacity to train one from scratch, I might require that every interviewee demonstrate their ability to handle a forklift truck as part of the interview process. This is because some people lie about their experience or qualifications on CVs and application forms. I would never find that out if I only interviewed every candidate and asked them questions about how good they think they are at handling this machinery, without asking them to demonstrate the skill live.

The best way to prepare for any aptitude test is to anticipate that it may happen during the interview process. As I suggest on page 111 in Chapter 4, your research phone call should reveal this if the recruiter hasn't already specified this in their email/letter inviting you to interview. Any skill or competence that you know is required for the job and will not be provided in initial training is a potential contender for assessment in a separate test format during interview. Expect that you will be given all necessary instructions for completing the test and clear expectations of the performance required. Know that everyone selected for interview will be asked to complete the same test under identical conditions, otherwise there would be no point in having the test at all.

By the time that you have reached this point in the book, you know that you are only targeting jobs that are the right ones for you, so you will be able to demonstrate the appropriate standard of performance in any form of aptitude test that you could meet at interview. They are part of the selection process for a reason, not at the whim of a recruiter and are designed to clarify for the recruiter a benchmark for every candidate's performance in an essential requirement for that role.

■ Assessment centres

These arrangements for mass interviews are used by large employers seeking to fill multiple positions, such as graduate training schemes or large-scale new employment, such as opening a new factory. At some point in the process, which will probably last at minimum half a day, typically one full day and sometimes two days, you will definitely experience a competence or evidence-based interview with one person asking questions and one person recording your answers. You may be asked to perform a range of aptitude tests, in some of which you will be required to interact with your competitors.

Every candidate moves around the same tasks either individually or as a small group, meeting a range of different challenges and tests that would be impossible to administer unless candidates are grouped together. For example, a very common test on assessment centres is to prepare a brief presentation on some topic relevant to the role and deliver it to a small audience that may include your competitors as well as the assessors. You might then be asked to lead a brief discussion about your presentation with the group. This inevitably also requires you to then contribute to others' discussions and react professionally with your peers. Panel interviews are also common at assessment centres (more detail on managing panel interviews on page 163) because they are a time-effective way of enabling senior managers to contribute effectively to the recruitment process and meet all potential candidates in one day.

This may sound daunting if you have never experienced such events before, but if you approach it as a very useful learning exercise, it can give you invaluable jobseeking experience. Even if you are not offered a post as a result of attending the centre, you will have learned a lot about yourself, your core skills, your target role and your target organisations. With so many people involved in assessing you, the organisation is likely to give you some detailed and high quality feedback after the event. Indeed many assessment centres also act as development centres for the selected candidates, giving them a personal development plan to start working on as they join the organisation. Another benefit of attending an assessment centre is the chance to be observed by a range of recruiters, maximising your chances of objective assessment. Even a short event gives you more opportunity to get a feel for the organisation than a one-hour interview. If you feel that a particular exercise didn't go so well for you, there are other opportunities to balance up your performance.

You also have the chance to display a wide range of your skills and competences in various aptitude tests. Often the 'softer' skills around communication, teambuilding and leadership behaviours are tested by these group activities. It is hard for recruiters to measure these softer skills just from words on an application form or a candidate's responses to interview questions about their perception of good communication. The function of role-playing or scenario exercises is to give the candidates a potential problem and observe how they go about solving it in real time. In any of the group exercises you take part in, expect to see observers seated around the edge of the room taking notes. These observers will be recording what people say and do during the exercise; usually one observer records one candidate. At the end of the exercise, the assessors have a record of everyone's behaviour throughout the process, which offers better evidence of how they display a competence in real life than asking their opinion of how they think they behave.

The key to handling assessment centres well and most importantly, conserving your energy for such a long time, is to ensure that you approach every activity with the same level of preparation as the interview. Having done your research, you will enter the process with a deep understanding of why the selection is structured in this way and what competences are being sought at each test. Consequently, relax and be yourself. In a very short space of time, you will stop noticing the observers and the exercises will start to feel far more natural. If you are not clear on any instruction, please check your understanding before the tasks begin. I could guarantee that at least one other candidate in the room is also asking themselves the same question. Over the next few pages, I shall outline some of the most common activities you might encounter at an assessment centre with some guidance about how to tackle them.

Presentations

Short presentations are common: you may be given advance notice in your interview invitation to prepare a certain topic or very little notice on the day, followed by some preparation time. This activity usually requires you to present your opinions of, or analyse information on, a relevant issue for that industry or job role. Often you will be delivering informally to a small group and may be asked to close the presentation with a question-and-answer session. You will be advised of the expected length of the presentation and it will be helpful if you could ask someone to give you a two-minute warning just before the end, to make sure that you cover everything that you planned to.

TIP

As a rough rule of thumb, it probably takes most people about ten times the length of the presentation to prepare it. For example, if I ask candidates to deliver a five-minute presentation, I'd try to allow 50 minutes' preparation time.

I prefer not to ask people in advance to prepare a presentation, so that everyone starts from the same point and uses the same resources.

The most common failing of candidates that I have observed working on presentations is that virtually all preparation time goes into the presentation at the expense of anticipating any follow-up questions. It is a similar problem to forgetting to prepare your own interview questions to ask. I have seen strong presentations wither away when it becomes clear that the candidate has not anticipated the need to follow up issues or answer predictable questions from their audience. Always consider why the recruiter has decided to test your presentation skills: any sales, training, customer service or media-based role has, at the heart of the role, the key requirement to deliver clear information appropriately to a selected audience. Even if this job will not need you to deliver formal presentations, a presentation task provides the recruiter with a wide variety of observable behaviours and demonstrations of competences. In setting you this task, I could observe how well you can:

- analyse information
- prioritise it
- summarise it
- adapt it for a target selected audience
- respond to a tight time deadline
- plan
- communicate effectively
- follow instructions
- listen
- express opinions
- persuade or influence others' views
- ask relevant questions
- respond to colleagues' comments
- understand the key 'hot topics' for this role or this industry

Notice that only the last potential criterion is directly assessing the content of the presentation.

> *"If you fail to prepare, you prepare to fail."*
>
> Well-known saying about presentations

If you are unfamiliar with delivering presentations, do not panic. As part of your preparation for an assessment centre, consider the range of potential competences that could be assessed by a presentation, as listed above and focus on those key competences for your target job. The process of creating the presentation and your delivery style could be assessed as important as the content, so anticipate that you might be formally observed during your preparation. The two most useful pieces of advice for less-experienced presenters are to:

- Keep it simple.
- Tell them what you're going to tell them, tell them and then tell them what you've just told them.
- If your task is to deliver a five-minute presentation, then allow:
  one minute to introduce your key topic in headlines
  three minutes to present your case, and
  one minute to summarise your key points.

Those five minutes will vanish at an astonishing speed while you deliver, which is why it is helpful to ask for a one- or two-minute warning. Frequently, assessment presentations invite you to use flipcharts as visual aids because they are the quickest way to generate some visual impact. Please only draw or write on them the absolute minimum necessary to support your key points. You cannot expect to cover five or six sheets of flipchart in a five minutes slot; your mantra is to keep it simple, so one or two sheets at maximum will serve you better. Try not to use the flipcharts or any other visual aids as your 'script'. I have endured far too many boring presentations consisting of a candidate simply reading out the words they have posted up as their visual aids. Visual aids are intended to be just that; your aids to highlighting the key points **for the benefit of your audience**. If they don't add value to your presentation, then don't use them. Your 'script' can only be notes to prompt you. If you attempt to write out a full script for your five minutes, you will end up talking to it and never making eye contact with your audience. That is, if by some miracle, you are able to write a full script in the preparation time allowed.

Check carefully before you start your allotted preparation time precisely what is expected of you in terms of content, delivery style, assessment criteria, format and who the audience are. If anything doesn't make sense, please ask the assessors. It is quite common for your live audience of assessors and fellow applicants to be asked to role-play a different audience, for example customers, if you were asked to pitch your presentation for an audience of customers. This would mean ensuring that you do not use jargon that customers are unlikely to understand and that you anticipate likely customer questions. If you are asked to answer a question in your content, then make sure that your conclusion states your opinion on the issue, so that you do actually answer it.

The content of any presentation will be directly relevant to the key behaviours, skills, knowledge or attitudes required for the role. You will always have an opinion to offer on the topic and the recruiter is always interested in hearing it.

You might be asked to address some topic that the organisation is famous for, or is directly related to the products and services they provide, such as:

What should excellent product reliability look like for our customers?

For some technical roles, you may be asked to comment on the organisation's products, services or procedures or even compare them with their key competitors. If you are asked to review the organisation's products, then one of the assessment criteria for the presentation is clearly to demonstrate how much research you have carried out on your target role and industry. I've seen some notably poor presentations that have exposed how lightly the candidate has researched an organisation that they claim to be very interested in. This is another huge advantage for the jobseeker who has followed the *Nail That Job* approach from the start of their job search; you will only ever find yourself attending an assessment centre for a job that you really want in an organisation that you really want to work for. By the time you are asked to make any presentation on some aspect of this role, you will come across as confident, knowledgeable and enthusiastic.

In-tray or Prioritisation exercise

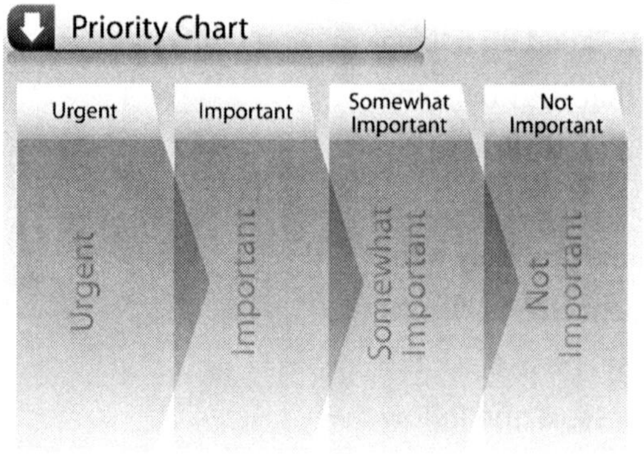

Another common activity in an assessment centre is an 'in-tray' exercise. You might experience this in either electronic or paper versions, as a mass of different sorts of information. The key purpose is to assess your ability to analyse a wide range of information, make decisions about which bits of information or tasks need to be prioritised and quickly plan a response to the issues that arise. These tests are often administered under very tight time constraints, so do not be surprised if you cannot complete all the tasks within your allotted time scale. Typically, the initial instructions describe a scenario of a colleague suddenly falling ill at a crucial point in a project with finite time deadlines. You have to open her emails and swiftly decide on what should be your next tasks to keep the project on track and consequently respond appropriately.

These exercises are carefully constructed so that detailed knowledge of the fictional job role is not required. You are being assessed on your ability to:

- analyse information
- prioritise
- connect information from different sources
- make decisions
- work to tight deadlines and/or under pressure
- communicate clearly in writing
- negotiate
- delegate
- work creatively
- solve problems

You will have to give a brief explanation of why you have chosen to work on the particular tasks that you select as important. This could be in the form of notes attached to each task you list, a report, or possibly a conversation with an assessor after you complete the exercise. The further you move into the task, the clearer the links between each piece of information will become.

Sometimes, new information is added part way through the exercise that changes something on your plans or makes the original issues that you have identified more complex. This is simply to test how you deal with changing priorities; a vital skill in many jobs in fast-changing environments. There will always be plenty of red herrings in the mass of information: your job is to identify them early so that you don't get side-tracked. Your key task here is to read everything carefully, keep calm and make a rough plan for listing your tasks.

Remember that urgent is not always the same as important but that different job holders or customers, suppliers, bosses, etc., will view the same event, task or request as:

- urgent and important,
- or important but not urgent,
- or urgent but not important,
- or neither urgent nor important, depending on their relationship to that event.

CASE STUDY

Read the question carefully

Check the instructions carefully before you start, to be clear about what is expected of you in terms of presenting your recommendations for action. Once I was puzzled to read a very scrappy and incoherent set of justifications from a candidate who had scored very highly across all the other assessment activities. We decided to offer her the job and when I gave her feedback, I discovered that she had simply misread the instructions and wrote her recommendations for action as a bullet point list of tasks instead of a full report. Assessment and time pressures mean that even strong candidates can prove themselves incapable of reading instructions.

Meeting skills and teamwork exercises

A common group exercise on assessment centres is for candidates to role-play a decision-making meeting. Typically, a group of five to eight candidates are given a brief about the need to make a decision about an issue or solve a problem. The task content, i.e. the decision to be made, may or may not be directly related to the target job. You may or may not be given additional detailed information about the role that you are expected to play. Observers will be stationed around the edge of the room to record what is said and done by each candidate. There will be a finite time allotted to the exercise and whether or not you have reached a conclusion, the activity will be stopped at the deadline: assessment centres have to be run like clockwork or chaos quickly follows. As usual with the *Nail That Job* approach, consider what the recruiter is looking for and why they might have decided that watching a group of candidates role-playing a meeting would give them the evidence that they need.

If I choose to use a meeting role-play activity in an assessment centre, I am probably looking for evidence around some of the following competences:

- ability to collaborate
- analytical skills
- communication skills
- creativity
- decision making
- flexibility
- generating rapport with a range of people
- innovation
- leadership skills
- listening
- negotiating skills
- observation skills
- persuading or influencing
- planning or organising
- prioritising
- problem solving
- selling skills
- strategic thinking
- teambuilding
- time management

Please don't imagine that in the course of a 25-minute observed meeting role-play, you would be required to demonstrate every one of these potential competences. You will know which are the most important for your target role and therefore which to concentrate on. A fairly common misunderstanding about these sorts of exercises is that someone has to 'take the lead', drive through their interpretation of issues and 'win' by forcing a vote from all the other candidates. In my experience these candidates do tend to be younger and male and consequently score poorly on criteria such as collaboration, listening and team building. If you do ever find yourself in such an exercise with someone trying to throw their weight around, then try to suggest a review or summary of decisions, or test the group thinking about how close you all are to achieving the task, or invite another quiet candidate to express their opinion (whatever action is appropriate at the time). Then you will score highly on all the competences around building teamwork, rapport and inclusive communication.

You might also experience a team-building exercise outside the decision-making meeting scenario. This is where a small group of candidates have to work together to complete a task within a set timescale; it might be researching a problem and presenting a potential solution, or collaboratively testing a job role related issue to recommend improvements. Whatever the task, apply your usual *Nail That Job* analysis to the exercise and consider what the assessors are looking for.

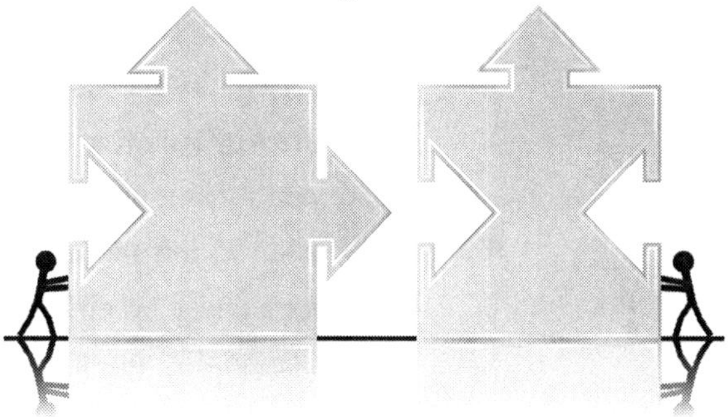

Any of the above competences are likely contenders for observation. Just like a meeting role-play, you are likely to be observed throughout the research or planning stage of the exercise and your behaviour here will be just as important as the final conclusions that the team comes to or the result or presentation that you produce. Expect to receive the instruction that everyone must take part in the report back, whatever the format, and expect to be questioned on the rationale for the decisions that the team made. Such exercises are clearly used when teamwork, collaboration and clear communication are vital competences for the role. All of the guidance above about dealing with an assessed meeting is also relevant here. Don't think that working with strangers to solve a problem is an artificial situation; the recruiters are interested in how you behave when you are asked to work with people you have never met before, build relationships quickly and achieve a task collaboratively. Somewhere in your target job's person specification must be the need to:

- Develop relationships quickly (with colleagues, customers, suppliers, or clients).
- Solve problems (creatively and/or logically).
- Present information clearly (to a range of audiences using a variety of media).
- Persuade and influence in a variety of relationships.
- Work as part of a team.

Setting a group of strangers a problem to be analysed and reported on is an effective use of time on a larger-scale assessment centre and would give the recruiters quality information on how you are likely to behave in a real work situation.

Role-plays

Role-plays can pop up at assessment centres, particularly if selling, customer service, negotiating, communication skills, creativity, innovation or teamwork are key role requirements. That core ability to generate productive personal relationships quickly is such a vital part of the sales role, that I would still be keen to test the aptitude or potential for selling skills, even if I am recruiting for trainees, where I am not expecting candidates to have direct selling experience. Personality questionnaires (more on these on page 164), will only take me so far in assessing someone's potential for a role that requires complex interpersonal relationships; I would like to assess your ability to lead a conversation through role-plays.

You might find yourself role-playing a particular situation with either fellow candidates or existing employees as your partner(s). For larger-scale exercises, professional actors might be brought in to play the part of disgruntled customers, potential sales targets, difficult employees, etc. If phone work will be large feature of the job, then you might well be using an audio link to a live person in a different room and should consequently expect this exercise to be recorded.

Some candidates allow themselves to be worried by role-plays in any situation. I have heard some applicants grumble that they are not auditioning to be an actor and clearly don't see the purpose of using them. Remember the recruiters' intentions; we are never trying to embarrass you or discomfort you in any way. We are trying to test out your potential in certain competences and the best way to do that might be to ask you to take on the role of your target job, describe a likely set of circumstances and observe how you deal with these. The *Nail That Job* candidate has prepared well, and is already familiar with the core competences to be tested. You will then relish the opportunity to demonstrate that you are already very capable of holding a difficult conversation, or persuading someone to your point of view. For example, if I was recruiting for the security officer from Chapter 3, I might choose to ask each candidate to demonstrate how they might persuade a disgruntled council taxpayer, played by another member of the recruitment team, to leave the public gallery of the council chamber. The candidates' verbal, visual and vocal behaviour (refer to page 139 in Chapter 4) would tell me a lot in just a few minutes about how confident and capable they would be about the trickier aspects of that job. That's all a role-play is.

Self-review

An intriguing additional task that the grapevine tells me is popping up more frequently recently (indeed, I have used it myself several times over the last year) is review of one's own performance. By definition the last task for a candidate, it is to write a brief report of how well they think they have done on each task. It has clearly stunned some candidates who have never thought that this analysis was their responsibility. I have found it very useful in giving us a feel for how well the candidate understands their own strengths and development areas they may choose to work on. I have heard of this self-review forming the kernel of successful candidates' initial training plan when they join the organisation.

Any *Nail That Job* candidate will not be at all fazed by such a task, as all your work in the first two chapters will stand you in good stead here. You will be well placed to reflect on your performance over the day or days and understand where you displayed your many strong abilities and honest enough to recognise when you perhaps didn't show yourself to best advantage. Treat this exercise as the golden opportunity that it is and complete your self-review as though it were your second chance at an application form or CV. Focus on what you know to be the core competences required and grab your last chance to stress how well you can display them at work.

Self-management

If reading the last few pages about what can happen at assessment centres exhausted you, then you are in good company. One of the key things to prepare for when you are invited to such an event is the sheer amount of energy that it consumes. The briefest of assessment centres will last at least half a day, many at least one long day and a significant number for two days. That is by any standards a long time to stay focused, listen well and be on your best behaviour.

Remember that these selection processes are expensive because they are also highly time and energy consuming for the recruiting organisation to arrange. Think through the consequences of this recruitment expense and effort: you will only reach an assessment centre after an initial sifting process, so you arrive there being considered worthy of further attention. Remember the advice in Chapter 4, page 144 about recognising how tired you are likely to feel after an interview: post assessment centre exhaustion is even more intense. You are on show to the recruitment team from the moment you walk into the building until the moment that you leave. Although not formally under assessment during coffee or meal breaks, you will still be informally chatting to members of the recruitment team and your fellow applicants. All those brief conversations will contribute to building up a subconscious impression in the recruiters of how you behave on a daily basis at work.

TIP

Make your mum proud of you

I have observed candidates losing tempers under pressure. This is why your behaviour towards your competitors must be scrupulously professional, polite and productive. If others lose their tempers or a rival chooses to sulk or argue in order to try to put you off, you must rise above it and continue to be gracious towards him or her. The assessors will notice and record it.

If the assessment process runs over two days and covers national posts, it is common for everyone involved to be given overnight accommodation at the hotel being used. Many graduate placement schemes continue activities into the evening, perhaps inviting senior leaders to a Question and Answer session before dinner. Over dinner you will still be expected to make polite conversation with your recruiters and competitors. Please go easy on after-dinner alcohol; you are still on show and the following day you need to give of your best again. If you take your cue from the recruitment team, you will notice that it is very rare for anyone to have even a small drink.

■ Panel interviews

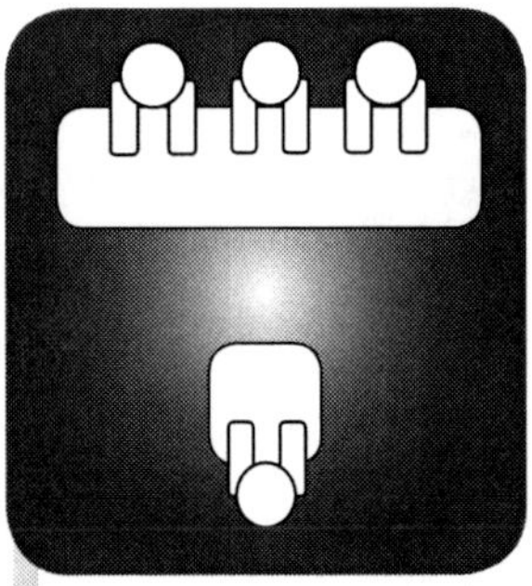

Panel interviews can take place either as part of an assessment centre or as a stand-alone selection process. Commonly they are used at the second or later stage of interviewing, when the highest scoring candidates after an initial sifting are asked to meet more, usually more senior, people in the organisation. They are also often used in the public sector as the only interview, where many different stakeholders have a relationship with the job role: for example, in teaching, a panel often includes a governor as well as senior staff. My definition of a panel interview is three or more interviewers: rarely will you experience more than four people interviewing you at once. The purpose of a panel interview is a time-effective way to enable a wider range of interviewers to ask you questions directly and therefore pool different viewpoints of you as a candidate. You may well have met one person on the panel at an earlier stage of selection: it is unusual to meet three entirely new interviewers on a panel at second interview.

Panel interviews tend to have a more formal feel than a one or two person interview as they are usually arranged with the whole panel behind one desk. One person usually takes the lead and acts as 'Chair' for the interview. They will introduce each interviewer by name and job title in turn at the start. Expect to repeat the handshakes and greetings three times at this point before everyone settles back to a seat. Focus on the fact that you will still make a positive first impression on all the interviewers, even if one of them won't be addressing you directly again for another 40 minutes or so. We know how hard it is to remember three names at once, so when I panel interview, I always ask my colleagues to repeat their names when it is their turn to ask questions. Try to remember the job roles on introduction, if not the names, because that will give you a steer for understanding their relationship with your target role and consequently the rationale behind their questions. When experiencing a panel interview in larger organisations you will probably be interviewed by a member of the Human Resources (HR) function, your prospective line manager and possibly their manager.

One person will start asking you questions. While they and one other interviewer nod and send all the encouraging 'I'm listening to you' noises, the third interviewer will be recording your answers and consequently rarely making eye contact with you. The roles of interviewer and recorder will swap as they move through their prepared questions. Some inexperienced candidates panic about whom they should be talking to: simply address your responses to the person who asks you the questions.

Occasionally, the other interviewers might break in to the flow by asking you a follow-up question depending on your last response. Remember that in any interview, the interviewer may choose to depart from their prepared script to clarify your last response or probe you further. The recruitment interview is not an interrogation. The questions could be divided up by the interviewers according to their personal relationship with or interests in the role, or they might choose to simply each ask one third of all the total questions they want to ask. The chair of the panel will take on the role of closing the interview and inviting you to ask any questions. By the end of the interview, I would expect that the *Nail That Job* candidate has worked out that there might be a most appropriate interviewer to direct a particular question to and will therefore direct it appropriately.

■ Psychological tests

According to legend, there are many recruitment questionnaires designed to encourage candidates to reveal their deepest thoughts about the meaning of life. They are applied on a daily basis to unsuspecting applicants. Most of these can be practised for on the internet, if only you could waste enough time on finding the sites to give you the right answers. Others claim that many of these tests are cobbled together from the coffee break questionnaires found in all sorts of popular magazines. Having read this far, you will know that all these beliefs are untrue. Let's start correcting a few myths.

If a recruiter wants to gain additional information about what motivates people at work, they could ask that question at interview. The well-prepared *Nail That Job* candidate has thought about their answer in Chapter 1 and developed it through Chapters 2 and 3. Few candidates can answer that question truthfully, because few candidates have the self-awareness to be able to genuinely know their answer to that question. Personality questionnaires, or psychological tests (both often referred to in the recruitment world as 'diagnostics'), are a way of revealing a candidate's preferred behaviours, motivations and attitudes to both the recruiter and the candidate.

These questionnaires can investigate a wide variety of preferred styles of behaviour, such as learning styles, teamwork or team roles, leadership, communication styles, information analysis, social motivation, influencing styles and so on. They are usually used for more senior or more complex roles when it is important to assess how well candidates can truly display the required styles of behaviour and how sustainable that is for them by identifying their preferred styles of working. I am thinking particularly now of those trainee sales roles. Candidates may express an interest in doing the job but they have no or very little experience to test whether they are truly suited to that role. They may genuinely believe, with only the experience of being customers, that they would enjoy sales. By asking everyone to complete an appropriate personality questionnaire, I can get a better idea of who would be more naturally comfortable in carrying out that role. These are the candidates best suited to my trainee sales vacancies.

There are no right or wrong answers to these questions; it depends on the core competences of the target job. You cannot practise for them, like an academic exam, so please do not waste your money on websites that claim that you can improve your performance by buying lots of examples. Of course you will learn many new ways of working as your career develops, but these questionnaires identify enduring patterns of behaviour that you learned early in your life and are now truly unconscious habits and preferences for you. It is extremely difficult to try to manipulate your answers if you think that you know what the preferred behaviours are.

You will be presented with a series of statements and asked to judge, either against a number scale or by choosing your preferred answer from a pair of descriptions, how likely it is that you would display this behaviour. Remember that these tests are always self-assessment: no one else has an input on your opinion of your own preferences. As you work through them you will realise that you are being asked similar questions by using slightly different wording or placing the behaviour descriptions in different situations. This repetition is part of the test's design to protect candidates from trying to manipulate it: perhaps 100 questions may assess ten aspects of preferred influencing styles, so there will be ten questions scattered randomly through the test that focus on each aspect. Another way of limiting efforts to manipulate your responses is to administer the test online and fade questions after a specific time into the next question.

Whether working on screen or paper, the same rules apply: consider each question carefully and make a decision fairly swiftly. Your first response is usually the one that instinctively is the right answer for you. Even if you read a pair of statements that would never describe your behaviour, you still have to select the least unlikely description of the pair.

You may experience personality questionnaires at an assessment centre, but they are now more common earlier in online application processes, where they are used as part of the screening to identify the candidates most likely to be comfortable using the required behaviours. Please be reassured by the knowledge that these tests can only be administered, assessed and the results fed back to you by specially trained recruiters. The tests have been designed by psychologists specialising in researching workplace behaviour and have huge historical databases behind them to identify statistical norms. Their purpose is to link the selected responses from any candidate to an accurate prediction of their habitual behaviour when carrying out the target role. Consequently they help to identify all the square pegs and all the round pegs. As the purchase and subsequent training needed to apply these tests are expensive, they are usually restricted to larger organisations carrying out large-scale specialist or senior recruitment.

■ Online selection processes

As suggested in Chapter 2 on page 51, the use of online selection, particularly for large recruitment exercises, is increasing. This is one of the core reasons for ensuring that you have a respectable email address and an online presence. By far the most cost-effective recruitment method for most medium and larger organisations is to manage the whole process up to initial interviews online. The vacancy is only advertised on the organisation's website: applicants are invited to complete an online application form and when large numbers of applicants are expected, there will be an online aptitude test, or tests, of some kind to filter out a shortlist. This ensures that the early filtering is achieved as cheaply as possible to generate an interview or assessment centre shortlist. Frequently, applicants are seamlessly directed onto a specialist online recruitment website, although it will appear to you that you are still interacting with the target organisation's website. Whether you access the application process directly or through agencies, you will most likely be shortlisted through specialist recruiting software that is searching for the key words in your application.

Be aware that some online processes might directly tip you onto a timed application form. This can catch the unwary browser who is just trying to register interest in a post, or research it further. Most processes enable you to work through the forms over time, allowing you to save different versions before committing to the send button. You will be able to set up a user account on the site, create your own password and then be able to manage your application to meet the required deadline. As you are now a seasoned *Nail That Job* applicant, you will have made good use of your research time and be ready to shine in your initial application, which will be full of relevant examples of your achievements, described using your target keywords that the software will pick out as worthy of more detailed attention.

More detailed attention may mean that you are invited to an interview or selection centre, or you may be notified by email that you now have entry to some further online tests. These next stage aptitude tests vary tremendously in content and scope, according to the required role competences. They could consist of any of the aptitude tests or personality questionnaires referred to above. Most of these tests will have a tight deadline; some may be able to be completed in stages.

Multiple-choice questionnaires are popular sifting tools here. Recruiters enjoy the flexibility of these sorts of tests, as some can be customised for each applicant. If you are comparing notes with a fellow student applying for the same training programme, don't be surprised if your memories of a particular questionnaire are different. Online processing means that different candidates could see a different question two, depending on their answer to question one. The benefit for the recruiter is that this is a cost-effective way to ensure that you are testing a wide variety of attitudes to the job, experiences, or competences, and ensuring that the most promising candidates reach interview.

Any and every aptitude could be tested at this point in the process; recently I have seen or heard of entry to the next stage decided by:

- a simple yes/no question:
  Do you have: the right to work permanently in the United Kingdom / a full driving licence / two years of customer service experience?
- a timed numeracy or verbal reasoning test
- a short piece of writing on your understanding of the term 'excellent customer service'
- a timed test of your hand/eye co-ordination
- a multiple-choice questionnaire testing your knowledge of the company's product range
- a keyboard speed test
- a timed data analysis exercise

In order to predict what tests may pop up for you online, consider how you would quickly screen out people who definitely do not have the potential to hold the role. *The Nail That Job* candidate reaps the benefits of carefully selecting only the most appropriate roles and consequently you will be able to anticipate how you might be screened online.

Golden rules for online applications

Ensure that you are not interrupted once you log onto your application account. If you are using mobile devices, you need to be in a quiet place with access to all your research notes on this job.

Read every instruction carefully before you start any exercise to check that you are quite sure about what is expected of you and how long it will take, or whether you can pause and save an exercise.

Use your knowledge of the organisation and the job description to target the key words to include in any application. Key words may be looked for in certain online tests, as well as on your application form.

Stay calm, even when you know that the test is timed. Most tests give you a progress update, e.g. 'Question 12 out of 20'. Some tests are purposely designed to be impossible to complete in the allotted time (recruiters are not sadists, they just want to observe how well you can perform the task under tight time pressures). If you want to change an answer, you will always be able to until you click 'next'. Most untimed tests allow you to review all your answers before you press send.

■ Telephone interviews

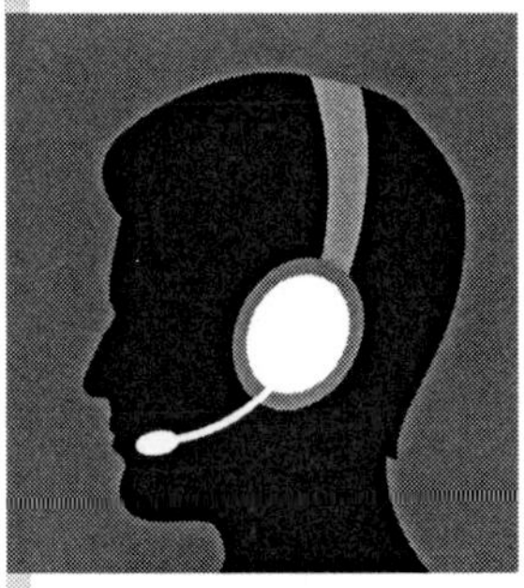

Like online screening, telephone interviews are becoming more common as a time- and cost-effective way to identify the most promising candidates to interview in person. If telephone work is any significant part of your target role, then expect to be interviewed over the phone at an early stage in the process. It is quite possible that any advertisement for a phone-based role asks you to ring a number 'for further information'. Beware: you are just as likely to find yourself straight into a screening interview with a recruiter, as speaking to an administrator taking note of your email address to send further details. Just as for your written applications, gather all your research notes and choose a quiet place to have this conversation. You might be finished in less than one minute just by giving out your email address to the administrator. The call may be your first interview and less-confident candidates might be finished in four or five minutes when the recruiter identifies that they are not ready for the role. Stronger candidates may may have their call closed 15 minutes later with the offer of a face-to-face interview. Some very inexperienced candidates do not even realise that they have failed the phone interview and assume that they were chatting to a friendly administrator. So long as you are prepared and ready to be formally interviewed, expect the conversation to follow an interview pattern.

First you will be asked for all your basic contact details to be taken. One of the vital pieces of research you need in front of you at this point is your core CV. The clue that you are experiencing a formal interview is when the recruiter then asks:

> *"So, tell me about yourself"*, or *"Tell me about your relevant experience of X"*.

You have practised your answer to this question on page 116 in Chapter 4. Suddenly, you are undertaking a formal interview but without any of the customary visual clues of a face-to-face interview. Expect an edited version of most of the questions from the list in Chapter 4. You will not be expected to cover your entire CV but respond to three or four key questions about your experience of the essential required characteristics for the role. Your research will have predicted which sorts of experiences or skills you will be asked to give evidence of.

Early on in the call, you might hear some of the simple, yes/no screening questions about work permits, qualifications or driving licences. For example, I may be recruiting for trainee hospitality managers and have decided that a vital experience for all entrants must be some bar, restaurant or hotel work. This becomes a yes/no question: if you can't give me an example of having even a brief stint of such work, I do not want to waste any more time on taking your application further. It is very rare for those who don't make it through a phone interview to be told at that point. If the response to a yes/no question puts a candidate in the 'no' heap, the interviewer will just professionally close the call as soon as is possible to stay polite and provide a contact point for them to send in a CV. Essentially, the longer your phone interview lasts, the more likely it is that you are heading for the next stage of the process.

Most people feel uncomfortable during phone interviews, as they have lost all those visual clues and ways of establishing a rapport with the interviewer. The more you have undertaken phone work in any capacity, the more used you are to making your voice work for you. Look back now to Chapter 4, page 141, Exercise 1 about generating the right impression and reflect on the words you chose to describe your vocal and verbal elements. You still have 45 per cent of your habitual means of sending the message that you are positive, confident, capable, professional, or any other adjective you choose. Those who spend most of their working life on the phone suggest the following tips to ensure that your voice works hard to send the right messages:

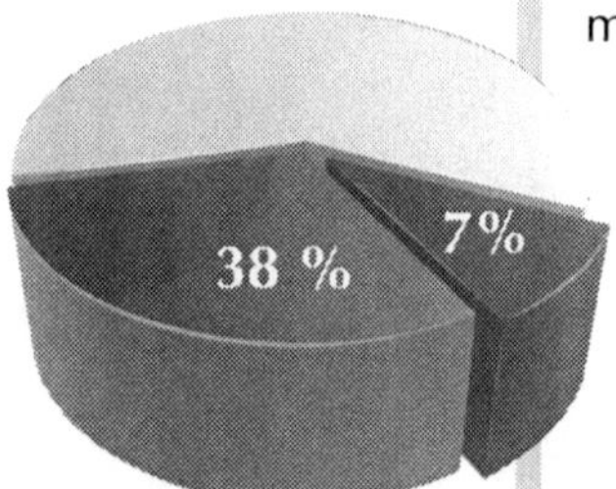

- Be prepared, with all your research notes to hand.
- Slow down to a speed slightly slower than you would normally use for face-to-face communication. This will help with any nerves too.
- Stand up to sound more confident.
- Remember to smile: even though the interviewer cannot see you, it is astonishingly easy to 'hear' the smile in another person's voice.
- Breathe deeply.

- If you do not understand the question, always ask for it to be repeated rather than stampede into answering the wrong question.
- Do not rush to fill the silence, take your time to think about the question you have just heard before you respond.
- Say thank you and check your understanding about what happens next at the close of the call.

The truly unprepared can get so flustered that they have no memory of the conversation and consequently are unsure about details: you will probably be invited to send in a CV to an email address within a specified time. The call may or may not be recorded. Recruiters are supposed to tell you at the start of a call if you are being recorded, but this does not always happen. You may hear the interviewer typing up your responses at their end, which should give you confidence that you are being listened to!

■ Second interviews

Second interviews can be a little tricky to manage. They are more common for more senior roles or jobs which need to relate to a wide range of other roles, where a larger number of people have an interest in meeting all the potential candidates. Sometimes unplanned second interviews arise when the first round of interviewing has not identified the candidate closest to the vacancy specification and the recruiter wants to explore new areas of experience in the strongest candidates to emerge so far. By the time you reach an invitation for a direct second interview, you are probably down to the last two or three candidates. Remember the golden rule of recruiting; every candidate is assessed against the job description and person specification, not against each other.

There is another form of second interview that is usual when applying through agencies: the agency runs a screening interview to provide the recruiting organisation with a shorter shortlist of candidates. In this case, entirely new people will interview you and therefore you may well hear again some of the questions that you were asked by the agency staff. This is not because the agency have not provided the recruiting organisation with a full report, it is just that they may want to hear directly some of your responses and probe them more deeply.

Essentially a second interview will always involve meeting at least one new person, answering some new questions and providing more detail about skills, experiences, talents or attributes that you have already discussed. Recruiters want to keep the process moving, so expect it to be within a week of the first interview, or at most, depending on the availability of the more senior people to be involved, inside two weeks. If you were anticipating a clear decision rather than a further interview, you may be feeling a little weary at this stage. It is vital that you arrive at your second interview feeling as fresh and as confident as you were for the first. Clearly the organisation is still very interested in talking to you further and finding out more about what you have to offer. Ask, if it is not made clear to you, who you will be meeting at the next interview in terms of job roles. To prepare effectively, look at your review notes that you would have completed after your first interview, as advised on page 145 in Chapter 4 and consider Exercise 1 opposite.

This checklist effectively creates your plan for the second interview and focuses you on preparing new evidence to talk about. Don't be disappointed if they only appear to want to talk about the same issues that you discussed in the first interview. You can still get in your new examples, so long as you judge it still to be appropriate, when you are invited to ask any questions. It's perfectly acceptable to say something like:

> *"Well I do have a couple of questions left, but before I ask them, could I just give you a few examples about my experience of X, as I think you will find it relevant?"*

Politely phrased and delivered as a question, they cannot refuse you and you will be able to take back control of the topic of conversation.

One experience that you may have at the end of a second interview is a direct question about your expectations of salary and this can take some candidates by surprise. In the public sector, there is no or very little room to manoeuvre; wage rates for jobs are publicly available, non-negotiable and directly linked to formal qualifications or years of experience. Anything to do with salaries in the private sector is far more opaque. The prepared, *Nail That Job* candidate has researched likely ranges of pay for this target role and is ready with a confident response, asking for a little more than

EXERCISE 1: Preparing for a second interview

	PREPARATION CHECKLIST FOR SECOND INTERVIEW
My highlights in the first interview were . . .	
I missed out/did not provide enough examples of these core competences . . .	
I might be asked for more information about . . .	
New issues they might want to raise could be . . .	
New highlights I could show off could be . . .	
I need to ask these questions . . .	

you might expect. Take your time when answering this question, never be embarrassed and focus on watching the reaction on the faces of either your potential line manager or the HR colleague present. Anything that implies the sucking of teeth, shaking of heads or sharp intakes of breath does not necessarily indicate that they think that you are wildly off the mark; it might just be a negotiating tactic. If they respond along the lines of:

> *"Well we were thinking that a package of about Y would be our expectations of the role . . .",*

this is merely an invitation to indicate their willingness to negotiate, not a request to close the deal there and then. Please then indicate that you are also keen to continue this discussion afterwards and that you would be happy to think about Y and ponder on it. The real negotiations will start when they ring you to offer the job and by then there will be little room to manoeuvre, but you may well hear something a little higher (or lower!) than you heard at the interview. Remember to review your Exercise 5 in Chapter 1, page 24 about your material, and your personal, social and emotional needs from this job and you will be clear about what you are looking for from this role.

LYING AT INTERVIEW

Sometimes candidates lie at interview or on application forms about their current earnings in the hope that they can start the salary negotiations at a higher point. This not only invalidates any job offer but is also a ludicrously easy fact to check when the new employer reads the P45 form completed by the last employer.

The bald truth is that as I write this, national wage rates are falling in real terms and employers perceive that they have the upper hand in the economic law of supply and demand in most labour markets. Bear in mind that recruiters have been known to pick the slightly more expensive candidate **if** they have been convinced that they have picked the right candidate. Just because you ask for what might be perceived as a higher than expected package, so long as it is not too far away from their expectations and you have demonstrated that you are the best match to the role, you might get it.

■ Informal interviews

Another tricky sort of recruitment meeting to handle is the informal interview, usually for more senior roles, unheard of in the public sector due to the potential lack of transparency and often held in all sorts of distracting locations. As ever, consider why a recruiter might want to hold an informal interview for a job. It might be due to the physical location of a candidate, or their working hours making it difficult to meet during the working day. A strong speculative application from a focused jobseeker may have landed in a gatekeeper's inbox and impressed them enough to spend a little time establishing a relationship with the promising applicant, even if there is currently no vacancy. You might request a short meeting with one of your networking contacts that evolves into an informal interview. These sorts of interviews are always exploratory, vacancies may not yet even exist, but someone is interested enough to want to find out a little more about you. If all goes well, you may be invited to a more formal interview or selection process.

Currently there are informal meetings being held right now in hotel foyers, high street teashops, posh restaurants, motorway service station cafés and business premises all over the country. Strangers and sometimes acquaintances, (connected by a myriad of past relationships as customers, clients, suppliers or past colleagues) are informally discussing the work experience and future career plans of one party. Agencies can meet promising candidates in a non-work environment if the timings and distances suit both parties. Sometimes, business meetings that start as an informal testing out of new projects between existing suppliers and clients might develop into testing out some poaching of key skills from one organisation to another. I have even heard of an invitation to a formal interview issued as a result of a conversation which began in a slightly stilted manner between two strangers over cheese sandwiches at a funeral tea.

The biggest challenge in handling an informal interview is to recognise when you are in one. You need to keep your jobseeking antennae on alert in all sorts of business situations in order to be ready. You need far more solid examples than just the development of your 'Meeting Prince Charles Speech'. If it dawns on you after a little while that the conversation seems to be sliding into more focused questions about your past career, you need to be ready with some clear examples of your many strengths and transferable skills. Once you have twigged that, then all the guidance in Chapter 4 remains valid.

Part of the intention of inviting you to an interview held in any non-traditional venue may be to encourage you to relax and be yourself or relax and be a little indiscreet. You might find yourself being probed about your opinions as much as your experiences: your views on anything from a competitor's products, to your assessment of your current boss, customers or organisation.

Most informal interviews are just that: a time-effective way of exploring your long-term potential without any commitment on the part of the recruiter. It is possible that you are being tested on your views on a range of issues that just might produce different responses in a formal meeting. The *Nail That Job* candidate is always ready to discuss their future career intentions honestly, professionally and productively in any formal or informal meeting.

To get a formal interview invitation out of such meetings is a true rarity. Your aim is to make a lasting positive impression that may not be directly useful to you for some considerable time. You may by then be holding a completely different job role but in the meantime, you have increased your professional network as a result of creating that relationship at an informal interview. It will probably be made clear that no current vacancy is available, but you may receive an invitation to other network meetings or contacts. Always close the meeting with a formal handshake, an exchange of contact details, and keep any promise to keep in touch.

■ Internal interviews

Many recruiters, including me, think that internal interviews are perhaps the hardest type of interview for both themselves and the interviewees. As a recruiter we can never win; the response from rejected candidates is always either:

> *"It was always going to go to an internal candidate and I was just making up the numbers"* or

> *"They were always going to give it to an external candidate, no one ever gets a chance round here."*

When you apply for a promotion within your current organisation, the barrier in your head is likely to focus on the fact that your track record goes before you. No matter how well you present your own achievements; you will be interviewed by someone who is aware of your 'less than good' days in this organisation.

From your first expression of interest in a vacancy, treat the entire process as though you are applying for a job in a different organisation:

- Brush up on your background knowledge of the whole business beyond your immediate function.
- Take your time over building the right CV to target this bigger job.
- Ensure that your behaviour on a daily basis explicitly demonstrates that you are capable of stepping up to the bigger role (this includes your relationships with any colleague who also applies for the vacancy).
- Check precisely who the interviewers will be and understand the detail of their relationship to your target role to help you anticipate the questions that they might ask.

Despite the fact that you may have been working for this organisation for some time, you will still be expected to talk about your perceptions of your key achievements and strengths, just like any external candidate. Indeed, recruiters become very conscious of the need to ask explicitly exactly the same questions of both internal and external candidates. This may result in an unusual situation where you find yourself describing a particular achievement of which your interviewers already have detailed knowledge. We are interested in your opinions of why you think that this example is a particularly strong one or why you chose to behave in that way in that situation. We are still seeking essentially the same information from you as from any external candidate: what do you think you have to offer that best matches the competences required?

Whatever the result of the interview, expect to be given detailed feedback on why you were or were not considered capable of the role. Most organisations want to see their 'home grown' staff develop into promotions but no manager is going to risk promoting an internal candidate who is not yet ready. There are no published statistics to indicate the percentage of total vacancies that go to internal as opposed to external candidates and I assume that the actual figure varies wildly according to industry and job role. What I do know is that recruiters are extremely keen to ensure that all internal applicants are assessed and are seen to be assessed on an equal

> *"The most useful questions for internal candidates concern their motivations. Why does this role interest them? Do they really know what they are getting into?"*
>
> PETER CAPPELLI, Professor of Management, University of Pennsylvania

footing to external candidates. This means being consistently clear about the expectations for internal applicants in terms of the standards required and the support offered. If you are not clear, then please ask for an informal meeting with someone in the HR function to check those expected standards as soon as you spot a vacancy that you are interested in.

Diplomacy is a key skill needed for working your way through an internal selection process. It is possible that you might be asked how you would improve things in this new role. You have to be ready with some positively phrased ideas that send the balanced message that you see opportunities for improvement, without appearing to sneer at the current or recent job-holder's efforts and achievements. That is a difficult tightrope to walk. You will probably also find yourself in direct competition with some of your existing colleagues. There is no way to keep the list of internal interviewees secret: arrangements have to be made to cover work while each internal applicant is being interviewed, so you will know who else is also being assessed very soon after you get confirmation of an interview. Remember that you are not being compared with each other: focus on matching the target role, not worrying about others' experiences, about which you can do nothing.

Sometimes organisations will choose to only advertise a vacancy internally and may even ask certain staff to apply for the role. If you are ever invited to apply, then give yourself a pat on the back: your track record has been noted and is approved of. Never assume that you are the preferred candidate, as pride really can come before a fall: you may be tempted to work on the application not quite as hard as you could or should. Even if you are not really interested in that role, then the whole exercise of applying will be helpful to freshen up your CV and give you useful job search experience. The benefits of keeping your CV fresh will be explored further in the next chapter.

CHAPTER 6

Staying employable throughout your career

By the end of this chapter, you will be able to:

- ***Leave your last job with dignity.***
- ***Make a positive impression in the early days of your new role.***
- ***Settle in to your new job quickly.***
- ***Ensure that you maintain a sustainable and productive professional network.***
- ***Review your evolving skills and experiences to keep your CV fresh and relevant.***
- ***Know how to stay employable for the rest of your career.***

Congratulations; either you have just opened an offer letter or email or have just put down the phone on your new boss inviting you to take up your target job. It will feel as though you have travelled a very long way since Chapter 1: you have worked very hard and with focus to sustain your energy and a new organisation's interest in you. Now you have a commitment to the job, which, even if it is not yet your dream role, is a clear step closer to that dream role.

> *"Your work is going to fill a large part of your life, and the only way to be truly satisfied is to do what you believe is great work. And the only way to do great work is to love what you do. If you haven't found it yet, keep looking. Don't settle."*
>
> STEVE JOBS, Founder of Apple

■ Tying up the loose ends

There will be a lot of boring administration to cover even before you set foot inside the door of your new job, but you will be led through this by the HR function or your new line manager. The paperwork will vary slightly, depending on your current work experience but expect to be dealing with most of the following issues.

Contact details for your referees, including phone numbers and emails are the most urgent pieces of information for your new employer. Immediately after phoning your nearest-and-dearest, your next calls should be to those referees to alert them. There is more guidance on breaking the news to your current employer on page 182; your new employer will agree with you a sensible deadline for you to have informed your current employer of your move and enable the new employer to ask your old ones for a reference.

Your new employer will send you two paper copies of your formal job offer and contract asking you to sign both copies and either bring one copy with you on day one or send it back before you start. This is a very important document to read and must be given to you within one month of starting the job. If you have any questions about any part of this contract, then contact your new boss or the HR function and ask.

Contract checklist

The job contract describes all the legal expectations of your role, such as:

- **job title**
- **core duties**
- **salary and its payment interval** (i.e. weekly or monthly)
- **start date**
- **hours of work**
- **locations of work**
- **holiday and sick pay entitlements**
- **pension entitlements**
- **notice period**
- **the job title that your job reports to**
- **any job roles that report to you**
- **any probationary period for formal assessment of your performance**
- **performance management arrangements**

There will probably be a reference to a Staff Handbook, which will be available to read on all sites or given to new employees as part of induction training. Handbooks list even more of the legal detail around expectations of behaviour in the organisation, such as grievance and disciplinary processes, recognition of trades unions, organisational charts, various policies that affect employment issues and dry but vital stuff like Health and Safety policies.

If you are starting your first job, you need to track down a copy of your National Insurance number: it was sent to you around the date of your 16th birthday. The government understands that dogs eat more than homework, so if you can't find it, then contact your nearest tax office or job centre, and bring with you every official document you possess that might help to identify you. This also applies if you are new to the UK and have not yet been given a National Insurance number. This may sound tedious, but you really do need this number before you start or in your early days in your new job, even if you are working part time and are not earning enough to have tax deducted. The number helps your new employers to deduct the right National Insurance and taxes from you (which could be nought) and record your contributions accurately.

If you are currently employed, either on your last day, or very shortly after you leave, your old employer has to provide you with a P45 form. This form records the total pay and deductions that your last employer recorded on your behalf and your dates of employment. Your new employers will ask for it on day one of your new job. If you are currently unemployed, your local benefits office or job centre will guide you through the paperwork needed for your new employer. You need to be budgeting ahead for this transfer between benefits and your first wage packet, which may well take over a month to reach your bank account. In the meantime your expenditure on travel and business clothes will rocket, so check that you can secure enough funds from friends, family or overdraft to keep you afloat.

You might need to make arrangements for other conditional parts of your offer, such as attend a medical at the request of your new employer. If you are applying for any job in financial services, then your new employer will ask to run a credit rating check on you. I have heard of conditional offers in financial services being withdrawn after such a check. Any job involving working with children or vulnerable adults requires a Criminal Records Bureau check and these are notoriously slow. Tediously, many public bodies interpret the law as requiring a new check for any new job, so even if you have had a CRB check within the last two years while working in Borsetshire, if your new job is in London, expect to have to wait for a new set of checks. Sometimes this may affect the planned start date for your new job, but there is no alternative for employer or employee with these checks. Also see the brief guide to the law for job applicants on page 198.

How to resign properly

Just as important as the paperwork, is to ensure that you leave your last job emotionally in the right way. You may be nervous about handing in your notice but it is a task that must be done quickly to clarify your leaving date. You should arrange to formally hand over or close your current work and leave a positive last impression. You truly never know if or when you may meet some of your current colleagues again in future new roles. The etiquette of handing in your notice is to speak directly to your current boss as soon as possible in a private meeting. Most job contracts will also expect you to hand in your notice in writing, so it seems a little previous to say something like:

> *"I have found another job and I'm leaving, here is my resignation letter",* and then hand over the letter already written.

The politest way to do it is to ask to speak to your boss privately, announce your news, formally ask for a reference and check your understanding of your official leave date. All sorts of wonderful HR calculations come into this leave date; you may have some holiday left to take and therefore might be able to leave sooner than you had anticipated. Expect your boss to want to know what your new job is and why you are leaving, so be ready with a polite and professional response. You don't have to give any detailed explanation beyond: "I fancy a change", or "I was offered more money". Only write your formal letter after this meeting, when your official leave date has been confirmed, so that you can write it in your resignation letter.

Should I stay or should I go?

It is just possible that your manager's response to your news might be to make you an offer quickly of increased money and/or new responsibilities. This is a huge spanner in the emotional works of your recent job search and needs a measured response. Your instinctive reaction might be cynical laughter and a loud declaration of freedom, in which case you have just burned all your boats. The seasoned *Nail That Job* candidate asks for clarification in writing of all details in this sudden job offer and considers it carefully overnight.

Assess the offer against your long-term objectives that you planned in your Chapter 2 SWOT and PEST analyses and your Chapter 1, Exercises 5 and 6 identifying your material, personal and social needs from your career. Unless the job truly does appear to be precisely what you are looking for from your dream job, simply ask for another polite and formal meeting with your boss the next day to reject the offer. I cannot remember ever hearing about anyone who accepted the invitation to stay and then flourished. I remain suspicious about the sustainability of any new role that is conjured up merely as a response to a good worker leaving.

You may be asked to have a formal exit interview with someone other than your line manager. The purpose of exit interviews is to hear the honest reasons for people choosing to leave jobs and use that information to reduce future turnover by changing things. I have conducted them myself and consider that the degree of honesty about the real reason for leaving is variable. Some people remain a bit suspicious, despite promises that the information will be handled anonymously. You might think that in the current job market, exit interviews are less common, but savvy organisations are always examining the reasons for people leaving and considering how to reduce turnover.

Whatever the length of your final notice period, it will appear to drag. You are looking forward to pastures new, while your colleagues are mentally and emotionally adjusting to your absence. While your brain is looking forward to new challenges, you will be expected to be working on completion and closure: tie up all loose ends, start to hand over work to others or even induct your replacement if that person is an internal candidate. You might have to ask a favour from your current employer if your new employer wants you to attend a key meeting or meet your new colleagues before your official start date. It is an odd set of relationships to manage when everyone knows that you are leaving, which is often a reason for offering 'garden leave' to the exiting employee: effectively being able to work out your notice at home.

■ Making a positive impression from day one

At last you are ready to start the right job for you. You have completed all the paperwork and signed and returned the required pages, know where you are going and who you are meeting to start the job. You might find it helpful to refresh your memory of page 138 in Chapter 4, because you need to reinforce the positive impression that you clearly made on your interview day. It sounds silly, but something as simple as having a pen and a small notebook, or the e-equivalent, to hand may help you send the message that you are organised and ready to learn.

Expect your first days to pass in a whirl of new faces and names, tours of unfamiliar buildings or sites, grappling with fire extinguishers on your health and safety induction training and the constant expectation from your new colleagues that all this information is going in on first hearing. Your early days in the role, perhaps up to your first month, are a precious resource that should be spent thoughtfully. Until your 'honeymoon' period is over, a new recruit has permission to ask all sorts of questions, both stupid and clever ones. Test everything that you don't understand or are not clear about and the most powerful question for you to keep asking right now is; " Why?" It is perfectly acceptable to ask to cover something twice if it does not yet make sense to you. Everyone in your new organisation, even those who are farther removed from your daily contacts in your job, can help you with answers if you ask.

The core activity of a new recruit should be to listen even more than ask questions: you have to learn a lot of different kinds of information quickly – technical, practical, cultural, factual, social and gossip.

Induction training to introduce you to your core duties, key colleagues or customer relationships, locations, processes and procedures lasts for as little as one hour to several months in more complex roles. Once you have triumphed over the paperwork and received the vital piece of plastic that allows you into your work space, you can start the process of settling in. Very early on, expect to have a formal conversation with your new boss about the performance standards required in your new role: a set of performance objectives will be drawn up and checked with you. These will form the basis of assessing your future work and probably also define satisfactory performance by the end of your probationary period or on completion of your key work. These targets could also represent the trigger for releasing any performance-related bonuses, so it is vital that you are clear about these core expectations of your behaviour. Remember that if you don't ask now, in six months' time you cannot claim ignorance of an expectation if your work falls short.

A fairly common source of anxiety for new recruits I work with, particularly younger people with less work experience, is uncertainty about how to manage all those new colleague relationships and clarifying the difference between social and professional links. It is extremely difficult to generalise across every workplace situation in the country, as each place of work develops its own social culture. As a rule, the smaller the organisation and the more homogenous the age range of the staff, the greater the expectation for everyone to socialise outside work, although you may have very different work experiences.

When you are new, your objective should be to cultivate positive working relationships with every one of your regular colleagues. You are not obliged to like them and spend all your free time outside work with them, unless you really want to. Neither are they obliged to like you and befriend you, even if you may have moved away from friends and family to take this job. As a *Nail That Job* success story, you will be operating within a wide variety of family and social networks and you are grown up enough to make your own choices about how you develop the right balance of new professional relationships.

In early days, it is probably a good idea to accept as many invitations to have lunch or visit the local pub after work as will fit into your personal plans, just to help cement names, job roles and relationships to your role in your head. You may hear a lot of gossip in your early days, whether over lunch or over work, but do not repeat it, or start any new rumours until you have many months of credibility within this organisation and a full understanding of how the grapevine operates there.

One potentially difficult relationship that you might find yourself managing is the internal candidate who also applied for your job. The overwhelming majority of such relationships develop into polite co-operation but are rarely warm. It is fairly common for the rejected internal candidate to move on to a new job themselves within a short space of time, whether a different promotion or to a completely new organisation. Your new manager should accept the responsibility of explaining to you in very early days that such a person is on the team and also should have given them appropriate feedback about why they were not considered a close enough match to the ideal. Recognise that they might be as uncomfortable about working with you as you might be with them. Always remain polite, professional and calm in all your conversations with them. In the extremely unlikely event that you hear an unpleasant or unhelpful response, you must tell your boss immediately a summary of the conversation. This is not about telling tales, it is about making sure that professional working relationships are maintained to the benefit of the entire team.

Be ready to be tired by the end of your working days as learning a lot of new information in a short space of time takes it out of you. Take care of yourself, literally, in terms of sleep, exercise, diet, commuting and home life. Try not to generate any other major life changes over the next year, such as starting or ending significant relationships, moving house or having a baby. There is such a thing as too many changes at once!

■ Sustaining your professional networks

Now that you have achieved your target role and are on a steep learning curve to deliver it, you may be tempted to leave behind all those professional networks that have helped you get here. Even if you found this job as a result of a direct advertisement, somewhere during your job hunt you had a thought-provoking conversation with another worker in this industry that helped you learn something. You may feel that you are now very busy at work, but if you do not return to any of those local meetings you attended, months could go by without you speaking to anyone in your industry outside your current organisation. That way, your learning starts to slow down. At the very least, the individuals who may have given you some very helpful mentoring advice while you were looking for your current role, deserve a thank you.

> *"The minute you start thinking that you've done it all, that's when you're in the rear view mirror."*
>
> CHRIS DE WOLFE, founder of MySpace

The key techniques to maintaining your professional networks are very simple:

- In the first month of your new employment, take the time to update your online personal profile in your chosen networks to reflect your new position.
- Within three months of having started your new role, make sure that you attend at least one meeting in your professional membership groups. While you are there, maintain the circulating network behaviour that you practised when looking for your job, *(see page 41 in Chapter 2)*.

Check with your line manager about your new organisation's expectations of using professional email addresses in public arenas and then follow the rules to the letter. Some businesses are sensitive about using your professional email address for networking communication. Recent case law suggests that misrepresentation of professional emails on public websites and forums may result in dismissal. If there is any doubt, stick to advertising your old job-hunting email address as your public point of contact or when contributing to industry-relevant online discussions.

Different industries and job roles have different expectations about how to continue your professional learning after initial induction. Online forums and industry specific blogs are useful sources of virtual networking that do not require any travel costs. They can be fitted into spare time both within and outside work and keep you in touch with relevant issues. Some technical roles demand fairly constant updating of knowledge and many professions have a range of official to less official online forums. If you are keen to raise your profile outside your current employer, then regular posts on these sorts of sites, or even developing your own blog, will help to keep your name visible.

As time goes by and you settle into this job, meeting colleagues outside your organisation to discuss hot topics in the industry will become habitual. This is vital for when you begin your next job hunt. You may be appalled at the thought of moving on if you have planned to stay in this role for many years. The fact remains that everyone's career plans and work needs evolve over time and at some point in the future you will be looking to move on. If you are unable to grow this new role into the next stage of your dream job, then you need to be starting your next job hunt (which may simply mean moving roles within your current organisation). In the meantime, the benefit of having stayed in touch with these networks is that both your address book and your industry knowledge stay up to date.

Keeping your CV fresh

Maintaining your address book is not the only thing to keep up to date. I strongly recommend the benefits of regularly reviewing your CV and updating it with your new skills and experiences. If you are planning to stay in this role for a long time, consider it the key tool for presenting your achievements at your annual appraisal in your current job. Jobseekers I keep in touch with tell me that by regularly reviewing their progress, they approach their first annual appraisals in their new organisations with confidence and pride. They can demonstrate to their boss what they have learned, how they have developed and the positive impact that they have had in their new role. All you have to do is to apply the CAR framework:

Challenge: what was the situation?
Action: what did I do to improve the situation?
Result: what difference did my actions make?

You have to decide the most helpful definition of 'regularly'. It depends on the pace of your job, any seasonal peaks, or natural pause points for specific projects. In the absence of these clear markers, a monthly review will be a good habit to develop. Your CV will always reflect your current performance and you can use it to clarify your worth to your current organisation. Simply set aside half an hour to reflect on your last month's work and ask yourself the questions opposite.

EXERCISE 1: Keeping my CV fresh and relevant

QUESTIONS TO ASK MYSELF	CV REVIEW CHECKLIST
What new skills, knowledge, understanding have I learned?	
What other situations, could I transfer those skills to?	
How can I demonstrate my recent achievements to my boss? CHALLENGE 1	ACTION RESULTS
CHALLENGE 2	ACTION RESULTS

This exercise is continued on following page

What am I most proud of?	
What do I need to develop further?	
Which of my preferred motivators is this job still giving me?	
How is this job enabling me to achieve my long-term career goals?	

Now that you have reviewed your recent work, consider how this information might develop your core CV and then adjust it if necessary. Most months, little or no change is needed to your core CV. However, if you ignore all this reflection until you reach your annual appraisal, it can be very hard to remember all your achievements and the full scale of your learning in this job. Make sure that you do yourself full justice in your appraisals. Your boss will continue to be impressed at your ability to review your own performance and notice that you are focused on your continuous learning. All you need to do is read your latest CV and ask yourself:

> *"Does this document genuinely sell all I have to offer my current or my next employer?"*

At this point you don't know who your next employer might be, but if the answer to that question is "No", then start adjusting.

TIP

Recording the compliments

Keep a file, both in paper and electronically, for all the informal comments of praise, thanks, and compliments that you will get from customers, colleagues and bosses. A simple, one line thank you email will come in handy when you review and update your CV and prepare for annual appraisal.

This is a quick and simple way to remember all the small and positive achievements that you make over a year: all you have to do is set up a Thank You folder in your emails and find a thin plastic wallet to file paper compliments.

If your answer to the last question in the checklist, 'How is this job enabling me to achieve my long-term career goal?' is a bit negative, then this is a signal that you should be looking at new options. You need to be either developing this job further, assessing potential promotions, or once again, looking to new organisations for the next stage of your career. The key benefit of being a *Nail That Job* success story is that you are all ready to launch your next hunt. You will find it helpful to refresh your memory of Chapters 1, 2 and 3 but you will no longer be starting from scratch. You will have an up-to-date CV that genuinely reflects all the skills and experiences that you have to offer, a successful track record of securing the right job at the right time and a very focused plan to nail the next right job for you.

The third vital benefit of regularly applying this little checklist is that review of your current work against your long-term career plans, turns you into a habitual career scanner. Your ears and eyes will always be ready to pick up the subtle signals that a job is or is not working for you and where you might seek out future opportunities. The vast majority of your career will be spent doing what you see as rewarding work and you will feel fulfilled because you are giving of your best, secure in the knowledge that you have nailed the right job for you. On the few occasions when you realise that you are outgrowing your current role, you will also be aware of this dissatisfaction quickly. At all times you will be in control of the next stage of your career.

■ Staying employable

No one can predict their full career from entry to the labour market to their last job before retirement. What we do know about modern labour markets is that there is less stability of tenure now than for perhaps the last few generations of workers. At the beginning of the early '80s recession, redundancy was a shameful negative experience for those caught up in it: many for the first time in their working lives. Redundancy remains a very tough experience from which to bounce back, but 30 years of repeated turbulence in labour markets mean that it is not such an unusual or even shameful incident as it was then perceived. Now we all know people in our networks who have been made redundant, some have experienced it several times. You need to expect and therefore plan for the fact that your job may not last as long as you would like it to in its current form. You may not be able to control global economic markets or politicians' budgets to limit the damage they inflict on jobs in all industries, but you can keep control of your chances of employability.

> *"Do what gives you a buzz."*
>
> TREVOR BAYLISS, inventor of the clockwork radio

Your huge advantage as a *Nail That Job* success story is that you have a highly developed understanding of your value in the market and how to keep that value current. Once you are settled in your new job, which, please note, you carefully targeted to suit your own values and your longer-term career plans, you will undoubtedly deliver good results for your organisation. You are a round peg in a round hole. Your long-term job hunt objectives should be to maintain that aim of matching into suitable work, never panicking into the first job available. You may learn to be a square peg in the future, and then you will search out only square peg roles.

Most HR professionals would advise the following as your best strategies for staying employable in turbulent times – they are set out below, in no order of priority:

- Take every opportunity (inside and outside paid employment) to keep learning new skills and competences and make sure you record that learning on your CVs and at your performance management or appraisal meetings.
- Stay current with industry developments by reading the trade press, joining relevant professional organisations and being aware of relevant technological developments in your field.
- Keep up your networking to ensure that you keep talking to others working in your industry and outside of your organisation.
- Stay focused on the core results of your role for your customers, clients, or end users. Be clear about what you do to make a difference and ensure that your end users and your boss keep hearing that message.
- Bring more solutions than problems to your boss: when you have to break bad news, tell them what you have already done to limit damage or improve matters.
- By regularly reviewing your own performance, you will identify skills or competences that you want to develop, so ask for opportunities to undertake further training and development and be clear about the benefit to the organisation if you secure this development.
- Clarify for your boss which values and personal motivators keep you giving of your best in this job and how your boss might be able to generate more for you by giving you new tasks.

Staying employable essentially means being able to demonstrate to your boss, colleagues, customers, your wider network – and above all, yourself – that you learn new competences throughout your planned and flexible career. These competences deliver measurable benefits for any organisation you choose to work in. A *Nail That Job* successful jobseeker has a range of strategies to do this instinctively. You don't need to rely on luck.

Enjoy the rest of your career,

Regards,

Sian Case

We'd love to hear about your progress in using all our *Nail That Job* hints and tips, so please tell us how it worked for you, by emailing **sian@nailthatjob.co.uk**.

Also take a look at **www.nailthatjob.co.uk** for more advice, ideas and success stories from jobseekers who landed the jobs of their dreams.

Recruitment Jargon Buster

Aptitude test

A short test of a specific technical skill required to deliver effective performance. It could involve typing, prioritising exercises, tests of verbal reasoning, numeracy, processing speeds and data analysis, etc.

Assessment centre

A series of selection processes taking place in one meeting, often involving interaction with your competitor applicants. The content and length of assessment centres varies widely depending on the activities used to assess candidates.

Blue-chip company

Large, high-profile company, implying that it has a reputation of being a sought-after employer.

Competence/competency

A description of a behaviour or technical or personal attribute required to do a job effectively or to a specified standard. Recruiters assess candidates' suitability for a role based on evidence of having applied certain competences in past work. Competency based interviews focus on asking you to give examples of having demonstrated certain competences or behaviours and are sometimes referred to as evidence-based interviews.

Curriculum vitae, usually CV

Latin for 'the race of my life'. A brief, neat and positively phrased summary of what you have to offer your next employer, presented electronically or on paper. *See Chapter 3 and also Resume.*

Discrimination: direct, indirect and positive

Discrimination means to treat someone or a group of people unfairly simply because of certain characteristics they possess.

Direct discrimination occurs if any part of the recruitment process actively excludes people with certain legally defined characteristics even though they may be perfectly suitable for the post. It is unlawful and has been for many years in this country and is truly extremely rare.

Still rare, but a little more possible, is **indirect discrimination**, where although all applicants are put through the same process, something about the recruitment process disproportionately excludes people in certain categories. For example, if the employer decides that only those candidates currently working full time should reach the shortlist, that indirectly discriminates against women, who hold most part-time posts in the national labour market.

Positive discrimination is also illegal and would happen if an employer decided to only shortlist and recruit women in order to redress a historical imbalance of very few women holding that post. Consequently they fail to recruit the best candidate if the best fit happens to be a man.

Also see Positive action, and the brief guide to legal issues in recruitment on page 198.

Exit interview

A formal meeting with someone, usually from the HR function in the organisation that you are leaving, intended to explore your reasons for leaving your job. It is conducted in expectation of hearing honest reasons why people are leaving the organisation and so helping it to improve any issue to reduce turnover costs.

Garden leave

A period of time when an employee is required to work out their notice by not attending work, i.e. gardening at home. During this time, the employee remains employed and their behaviour is often restricted by the employer, for example, they would not be allowed to set up any sort of competing business, work for a competitor or contact customers.

Continued on following page

Headhunter

A specialist recruiter working on behalf of organisations looking for senior people who may not be actively searching the job market but whose skills are in high demand.

Human Resources or HR

A title given to individuals, or departments in larger organisations, responsible for the recruitment and development of all the people who work for that organisation. They will lead most recruitment activities in medium and larger organisations, supporting line managers, who will be the managers responsible for your work once recruited.

Job description

A list of the essential functions of a role, detailing what the jobholder is paid to do. It often includes information such as who the jobholder reports to, titles of any roles that report to the jobholder, and key outcomes required of the role. This list of tasks determines which core competences are required for the Person specification, *see right*.

Jobs boards

Websites that advertise jobs usually under locality or industry headings. They are effectively the online shop window for recruitment agencies.

Key words/ key word searcher

Computer search tools are often used in large-scale recruitment exercises for initial sifting of large numbers of candidates. They are programmed to look for certain key words within a CV or an application form that show that an applicant has the relevant skills and experiences. The key to passing computerised sifting is to ensure that your research identifies which key words are appropriate to include in your application. Many programs reject applications where the key words are mentioned inappropriately or too frequently: you have to judge what that means for your application.

O.T.E.

On-target earnings, indicating that the salary package has a significant element of commission or bonus pay.

Person specification

A description of the skills, knowledge, attributes, experience and qualifications delivered by an ideal jobholder. Frequently these characteristics are subdivided into 'essential' and 'desirable'. The person specification is used to measure all applicants against the ideal personal characteristics, so it determines the choice of assessment activities for the recruitment process. *Also see Job description.*

Positive action

Positive action is lawful. It describes any activity by an employer explicitly designed to increase numbers of applications from traditionally under-represented groups. For example, an employer could offer special training just for female staff designed to encourage a higher percentage of female applicants for future promotions. Any further activities designed to boost their chances once all applications have been received would become illegal, positive discrimination.

Probationary period

An initial employment period subject to formal assessment, which must be completed to a required standard for a permanent contract to be confirmed or a specific pay rate achieved. The length of a probationary period varies greatly, depending on the job demands, qualifications and entry routes.

P.R.P.S.

Profit-related pay scheme: some part of the salary package is linked to an organisational performance-related bonus.

Psychometric and personality tests or diagnostics

Questionnaires which ask you a series of questions, using slightly different wording, about your thoughts and opinions of various work-related situations. The results show the pattern of your attitudes, beliefs and preferred behaviours that demonstrate your default styles of communicating, decision-making, teamwork, leading others or other relevant interactive skills. Most of these sorts of tests require the recruiter to have undergone specialist training to use them and give you feedback.

Reference/referee

Recruiters expect you to be able to offer at least two references from people who know your work well enough to comment on your performance and are not related to you. References can be described as 'character' references if the person commenting on you has not worked with you. At least one of the references should be from your last employer. Referees will not be contacted until a recruiter has decided to offer you a job, so you give your new employer permission to contact your current employer. All job offers are conditional on the production of satisfactory references. Please keep your referees up to date on the progress of your job search. *Also see Testimonial.*

Remuneration

The whole of your salary package, i.e. the money you are paid plus all your benefits, such as pension, bonus, overtime and discounts etc.

Resume

French for 'summary'. *See Curriculum vitae, page 195.* Commonly mentioned in recruitment literature from European or North American organisations and tending to be briefer than CVs.

Screening interview

The first interview in usually a pair of interviews, which is focused on screening out the less likely candidates in order to generate a shorter list for deeper inspection at a second interview. In large-scale recruitment exercises, an initial screening interview is often given over the phone or through online questions to bring numbers down towards a manageable number for face-to-face interviewing. Screening interviews could also be run by a recruitment agency who then recommend a smaller number of applicants go on to meet the recruiting organisation directly.

Testimonial

An open reference written to praise the work or character of an applicant generally, without any reference to their suitability for a specific role. Testimonials may be shown to a recruiter in addition to, not instead of, formally requested references.

Transferable skills

Skills learned in one job that are applicable to different jobs or different contexts. For example the technical skills required to be a competent plumber remain relevant only in the plumbing industry. However, the customer service skills of dealing effectively with people who may be flooded, or otherwise distressed, could be used in any situation that requires dealing with stressed customers and so are transferable.

USP or Unique selling proposition

This is your unique mixture of skills, experience, knowledge and understanding that you have to offer the workplace. You must make sure that in all your approaches to potential employers, they are fully aware of what your unique selling proposition is.

A BRIEF GUIDE TO THE LAW FOR JOB APPLICANTS

Even before you start work at your target organisation, the law offers you protection against unfair treatment as a job applicant. This section outlines the key pieces of legislation that relate to recruitment and I need to stress that I have no legal qualifications. I am summarising my understanding of the core legal issues that I keep in mind from the design of any recruitment process onwards, to ensure that I can genuinely say that I have treated every applicant fairly.

The most important thing to remember is that recruiters are expressly interested in acquiring the widest possible range of all good candidates, beyond their legal obligations. Consequently, it really is very rare to come across recruitment processes that break the law: unfair treatment of some or one candidate(s) is not only unlawful, but risks missing the best candidate, so is poor practice. If you do think that you have been treated unfairly as a result of possessing any of the characteristics listed below, then one of my rare website recommendations will help you towards better qualified advice: **www.citizensadvice.org.uk**, the excellent Citizens Advice Bureau. I would ask you to consider though whether it is a good use of your jobseeking time to chase an organisation that has already rejected you. There will be other organisations out there more worthy of your talents.

The Equality Act 2010

This act tidied up a long list of historical anti-discrimination legislation. Essentially it is unlawful for an employer to treat you unfairly during the recruitment process in any way due to any of the following:

- age
- disability
- gender re-assignment
- marriage and civil partnership
- pregnancy and maternity
- race
- religion or belief
- sex
- sexual orientation

Unfair treatment includes the failure to make reasonable adjustments in order to accommodate a person's disability. This Act also prevents prospective employers from asking applicants questions about their health, including whether they are disabled, until after the applicant has passed all the other selection procedures and therefore has demonstrated that they meet the non-health job requirements.

A recruiter must also ensure that they do not treat unfairly any applicant who is associated with anyone holding these characteristics. An example of this could be if the best-fit candidate mentions that their partner is disabled, so the recruiter assumes that they may not be able to fulfil the hours of work due to caring responsibilities and decides not to offer them the job.

The Act also applies to existing employees who are seeking promotions or access to development opportunities, i.e. internal candidates.

Pre-employment checks

Under several different pieces of legislation, recruiters have rights to, and indeed in certain situations, legal obligations to make specific checks on prospective employees.

All employers must check and make copies of specific documents as their duty to confirm whether the new recruit is eligible to work in the UK. All this paperwork must be seen and recorded by the employer before the new recruit starts work. If employers are found to be employing workers without the right to work, they will face large fines.

Anyone working with children and vulnerable adults must undertake a Criminal Records Bureau Check and be registered under the Vetting and Barring Scheme on the lifelong Independent Safeguarding Authority (ISA) registration. Essentially the CRB checks applicants against the national record of all criminal convictions. An ISA registration, checkable online by the prospective employer, shows that there is no known information that an individual presents a risk to working with children or vulnerable adults and this information is continuously monitored and updated by the ISA.

The Rehabilitation of Offenders Act 1974 enables criminal convictions to be 'spent', or ignored, after a specified 'rehabilitation period'. The length of any rehabilitation period varies according to the age the person was at the time of the offence (either under or over 18) and the nature of the sentence given. This act is designed to allow people with few or minor convictions to effectively leave them behind and with a few occupational exceptions, once the rehabilitation period is over, an applicant need not disclose these historic offences. Custodial sentences of more than two and a half years can never become 'spent' and must therefore always be disclosed as part of the application. Recruiters are responsible for ensuring the secure handling of all such sensitive information about an applicant and that only those people directly involved with the recruitment should see it. Any criminal record should be carefully assessed by the recruiter for its relevance to the job concerned, to allow an objective recruitment decision to be made.

Employers have no obligation to provide a reference for employees, but if they do so, they have a duty of care to make it sure it is accurate.

Lightning Source UK Ltd.
Milton Keynes UK
UKOW020131190512

192855UK00001B/2/P

9 780956 085993